WAVES
of
TIME

Published by Trident Press Ltd
Text: © Trident Press 1998
General Editor: Peter Hellyer
Production Editor: Paula Vine
Text Editor: Gabrielle Warnock

Contributing authors:
D.T. Potts
J.A. Elders
P. Hellyer
P.J. Vine
S. Aspinall
S. Howarth
A.C.F. David

Photographs:
© Trident Press & acknowledged
photographers and agencies
Layout & Design: © Trident Press 1998

The publishers wish to acknowledge
with thanks the support of the
Ministry of Information and Culture,
United Arab Emirates in producing
this book.

Further information on the
United Arab Emirates is available from
the Ministry of Information and Culture,
PO Box 17, Abu Dhabi, UAE
Tel: (9712) 453000
Fax: (9712) 450458
e-mail: mininfex@emirates.net.ae

On the World Wide Web at:
www.uaeinteract.com
www.the-emirates.com
www.lesemirats.com

British Library Cataloguing in
Publication Data.
A CIP catalogue record for this book is
available from the British Library.

ISBN: 1-900724-20-0

Trident Press Ltd.
2-5 Old Bond Street, London W1X3TB
Tel: 0171 491 8770
Fax: 0171 491 8664
www.tridentpress.com
E-mail: info@tridentpress.ie

24/07/23

WAVES of TIME

The Maritime History of the United Arab Emirates

TRIDENT PRESS

"They have the 'compass' and they have lines describing miles and their rhumbs are eight heads of al-Zauj and between these are eight more. All the sixteen have names of stars in the Egyptian and Maghribi languages... .

"We use 32 rhumbs and we have tirfa, zam and qiyas (measurements of star altitude) but they are not able to do these things nor can they understand the things which we do although we can understand what they do and we can use their knowledge and travel in their ships. ...We can easily travel in their ships and upon their sea so some have magnified us in this business and look up to us for it. They acknowledge that we have the better knowledge of the sea and its sciences and the wisdom of the stars in the high roads of the sea, and the knowledge of the division of the ship in length and breadth. For we divide the ship in length and breadth according to the compass rose and we have measurements of star altitudes. They have no similar division or any means of dividing from the prow of the ship to guide themselves; neither do they use star altitude measurements to guide them when they incline to the right or left. Hence they have to acknowledge that we know best in that."

Ahmed Ibn Majid (c.1432-c.1506)

Contents

Nieuwe Pascaert van
OOST INDIEN
Verthoonende hen van C. de Bona
Esperança tot aen het Landt van Espe
Geleyt op Waß ende Graeden en van
Veel fouten verbetert
Met Privilegie voor 15 Iaar

A S I

P E R S I A

C. BARDAMASSER.

EGYPTEN.

YEMEN;

Ormus.

Guadel

M O

Gouzeratte

CAMBAIA.

ARABIA FELIX

Fartaque

A F R I

C Æ

MAGADOXA

Sint de Babelmandt

C. Dofar

Linea Æquinoctialis.

C. Camorin

Cole

A B I S-

MESANDE

MOMBASA.

Ilha do Abrodos

Us tres Irmaons

Pernabaque

P A R S

Q U I S O Q

Baixos de Patras

Abrolus

As Chagas

I.d. Diego Garcia

Comoro

I.d. Roquepis

Pebourog

S I N A

MOZAMBIQUE

I.d.S.Maria

Cergados
Carayas

San Bromdas

SOFFALA

Diego Rodrigos

Tropicus C.

Maritime Beginnings

Daniel Potts

NATIONAL IDENTITIES ARE LIKE CRYSTALS. They are multi-faceted, not one dimensional. In this regard the United Arab Emirates is no exception. It is a land of many identities which may be defined according to a wide array of political, economic, socio-cultural, historical, geographical and other criteria. One of the most obvious geographical criteria by which the UAE and its forerunner, the Trucial States, has identified itself and been identified by others is the fact that the country is bounded on two sides by important saltwater bodies, the Arabian Gulf and the Gulf of Oman or Arabian Sea. Thus, with a mainland coastline nearly 800 kilometres long, the UAE must, in any geographical classification, be considered a maritime nation. Yet this categorisation of the UAE raises many historical questions. How important was the sea in the remote past of the country? How significant was the maritime orientation of the region's early inhabitants? How is the marine heritage of the UAE manifested in the country's archaeological record? These issues will be addressed in the following two chapters.

One of the great puzzles of archaeology in the UAE is the absence of any settlement dating back to the last glacial age or Pleistocene era, an absence which stands in stark contrast to the situation elsewhere in the Arabian peninsula. Although the reasons behind the absence

Contact with southeastern Iran and Baluchistan resulted in the import of decoratively painted black-on-grey ware canisters such as this one from the tomb at Tell Abraq.

of Palaeolithic occupation in the UAE have yet to be thoroughly researched, preliminary indications are that adverse climatic conditions during the last glacial era, with harsh weather and winds strong enough to transport sand, would have made living in the region at that time comparable to picnicking in a sandstorm for much of the year. It is little wonder then that there is no evidence of the presence of man's earliest ancestors, the hominids, in the Emirates. Man, *Homo sapiens*, only began to infiltrate the region after an amelioration of the climate during the Early Holocene era brought about in large part by an increase in rainfall caused by the northward displacement of the summer monsoon, itself due to a slight shift in the earth's orbit.

Thus, although seemingly late in comparison to many other parts of the world, the human colonisation of the UAE does not pre-date c. 5000 BC. The question is who were those early colonists and where did they come from? Although the evidence is meagre, it seems likely that the earliest colonists came, with their stone tools and their herds of domesticated sheep and goats, out of the North Arabian/Syrian desert milieu where the stone tool tradition shows links with eastern Arabia (the blade-arrowheads of Qatar being the earliest stone tools found anywhere in the area).

Now what do desert herders with pressure-flaked stone tools have to do with early marine exploitation? Desert herders do not sound like potential early fishermen or coastal denizens, however it was the particular geographical and climatic characteristics of the UAE which played a decisive role in shaping the pattern of settlement along the coast. Permanent prehistoric settlement was just as possible on the coasts of the UAE as in the interior, yet recent history suggests that the combined exploitation of both the coast *and* the interior on a seasonal basis may be the key to understanding early settlement in the region. In many parts of Oman and the UAE groups traditionally migrated seasonally from the interior (where they tended their gardens and date groves in the summer while escaping the oppressive heat and humidity of the coast), to engage in fishing and shellfish gathering on the coast for the winter. Thus, it would be artificial and incorrect to classify the members of such groups as 'fishermen' as opposed to 'herders'. Even where groups appear more specialised economically, there is a great deal of interaction between coastal and inland populations, each exchanging its particular products (e.g. dates from the interior, dried fish from the coast) for those unavailable locally. The ubiquity of stone tool types of the Arabian bifacial tradition on both coastal (e.g. Merawah, Hamriyah, al-Madar, Jazirat al-Hamra) and inland sites (e.g. Khatt, Al-Ain) suggests that, as a population, the ancient inhabitants of the coasts, desert and mountains of the UAE were one and the same, and the environmental potential of both the coastal and inland habitats was absolutely clear to the region's earliest colonists.

What were the specific resources provided to those early inhabitants by the coastal biotopes of the UAE?

Marine resources and coastal geomorphology

The marine environment is anything but monolithic. Tidal flats, lagoons, shallow water, deep water – each is a unique biotope inhabited by different species of flora and fauna, the exploitation of which sustained the region's earliest inhabitants. The nature of those archaeological sites found along the UAE coast is equally varied, reflecting both the different sorts of fauna exploited and the different activities which took place. Large shell concentrations or middens at Hamriyah, al-Madar or Jazirat al-Hamra indicate the gathering and shucking of vast quantities of shellfish in prehistoric times, principally the bivalves *Anadara ehrenbergeri*, *Barbatia* sp., *Marcia hiantina*, *Pinctada radiata* and *Saccostrea cucullata*, and the gastropods *Murex* (*Hexaplex*) *kusterianus*, *Terebralia palustris* and *Turbo coronatus*. This range of species, however, gives a misleading impression of the variety of shellfish consumed on the coastal sites. At al-Madar, for example, almost two-thirds (63 per cent) of the shellfish recovered from the excavations and corings undertaken there were oysters (*Saccostrea cucullata*). Moreover, the high frequency of mangrove root-impressions on the al-Madar oysters clearly points to their having originated in a lagoonal environment.

In addition to shellfish, fish, including emperors (*Lethrinus* sp.) and porgies (Sparidae indet.), were caught in very small numbers and dried or eaten in the fifth millennium at al-Madar, as were crabs. Both types of fish inhabit the shallow waters along the Gulf coast, and the examples recovered were those of small individuals which normally stay close to shore. This would suggest that the inhabitants of al-Madar were not capable of venturing into the deeper waters of the Gulf at this stage. The presence of net sinkers at the site does not necessarily suggest that nets were being used for deep sea fishing, for these could just as easily have been cast from the beach into the shallow offshore waters. On the other hand, a series of sites with bifacially retouched stone tools as well as shell middens similar to those of al-Madar have been discovered on several of Abu Dhabi's offshore islands, including Dalma, Ghagha' and Merawah. The Abu Dhabi island sites are particularly interesting because they suggest that some sailing capacity existed amongst the inhabitants of the Lower Gulf at this stage. Even if, as is possible, sea levels were somewhat lower than they are today, some of the islands further offshore, Dalma being one important possibility, must originally have been populated by groups from the mainland.

In addition to Arabian bifacial tools, net sinkers, imported pottery from Mesopotamia, and beads characterise the inventory of finds from these island sites. In the period c. 4500–4000 BC the coasts and islands of Kuwait, eastern Saudi Arabia, Bahrain, Qatar and the UAE were visited by Mesopotamian sailors who brought with them a distinctive type of painted pottery named after the site of Tell al-'Ubaid in southern Iraq. In the UAE both painted and plain 'Ubaid sherds have now been found at a number of sites including Jazirat al-Hamra in Ras al-Khaimah; al-Madar in Umm al-Qaiwain; Hamriyah in Sharjah; and Dalma island off the west coast of Abu Dhabi. While the coastal population of the UAE had not yet begun to make its own pottery, contact with Mesopotamia was apparently no inducement to take up the practice, and it would be almost 1500 years before a local ceramic industry emerged in the region.

Other coastal shell middens, similar to those of al-Madar, exist on the East Coast of the UAE at Kalba, site of what is currently one of the largest stands of mangrove in the UAE. The coastal occupation of the East Coast is likely to have differed somewhat from that of the Gulf Coast, for the stone tool types characteristic of the coast of Oman belong to a prehistoric industry which diverges from that found further north in Saudi Arabia, Qatar and the UAE.

Moving from the fifth to the fourth millennium we find some important differences in maritime

The Waves of Time

adaptation. During the fourth millennium marine mammals like the dugong (*Dugong dugon*) and reptiles such as the green turtle (*Chelonia mydas*) were caught and butchered at a site on the island of Akab in the Umm al-Qaiwain lagoon. Both animals are absent on earlier sites. A thousand years later the number of marine species 'on the menu' had increased even further, although not uniformly at all sites on the coast. On Umm an-Nar island near Abu Dhabi dolphin (*Delphinus* sp.), rorqual (*Balaenoptera*), green turtle (*Chelonia mydas*), shark (*Sphyrna* sp.), sawfish (*Pristis* sp.) and stingray (?*Dasyatis*) were exploited, as were a number of water fowl, including duck (*Anas querquedula*), flamingo (*Phoenicopterus* aff. *ruber*), Socotra cormorant (*Phalacrocorax nigrogularis*) and possibly the giant heron (*Ardea bennuides*). The lagoons of the UAE have always been home to a wide variety of crustaceans which have in turn provided food for a vast number of wintering and passage birds. Moreover, the beds of seagrass which characterise the lower portions of the coastal lagoons

Socotra cormorants breeding on an inshore island in the UAE.

Sea turtles began to appear in the diet of the region's inhabitants in the fourth millennium.

provide a rich feeding ground for sea turtles. Nevertheless, in spite of the variety of marine fauna, to which terrestrial species must also be added (e.g. domesticated cattle, sheep and goat, as well as wild oryx, gazelle and camel), it is important to stress that green turtle and dugong made by far the greatest contribution to the diet of the site's ancient inhabitants. The situation was not dissimilar on the small island of Ghanadha, situated between Abu Dhabi and Dubai. There the small percentage (c. 10 per cent) of birds and such terrestrial mammals as camel, cattle, oryx, gazelle and goat were far outnumbered by the remains of dugong, fish and turtle.

Moving further north to the site of Tell Abraq on the border of Sharjah and Umm al-Qaiwain we find the largest faunal sample from anywhere in the UAE. Since all fish and animal bone as well as shellfish from the excavation were kept, it was possible to identify no fewer than 41,546 bones from four seasons of excavation (1989–1993). For purposes of faunal analysis the material has been divided into three main periods corresponding to the so-called Umm an-Nar period (c. 2300–2000 BC), the Wadi Suq period (c. 2000–1300 BC), and the Iron Age (c. 1300–300 BC). Although percentages of different species found at the site vary through time, it is generally true that while terrestrial domesticates, such as sheep, goat and cattle, formed the most important source of protein in the late third millennium, contributing c. 75 per cent of the dietary requirements of the ancient inhabitants, dugong, sea turtle, cormorant and fish gradually increased in importance, especially during the second millennium BC. Although the final report on the fish remains is still in preparation, it seems clear that, in comparison with the populations of Umm an-Nar and Ghanadha, the ancient people of Tell Abraq relied much more on terrestrial fauna, like their counterparts at the inland oasis site of Hili 8, than on fish, shellfish, crustaceans or marine mammals. At the second millennium settlement of Shimal in coastal Ras al-Khaimah, on the other hand, fishing seems to have played a more important role early in the site's existence (c. 1600–1300 BC), while terrestrial fauna became more important towards the end of the occupation there. With more than 48 species represented in the faunal inventory from the site, the most important were the jacks or horse mackerel (*Caranx* sp.), examples of which often reached 80 centimetres in length, followed by tuna (*Thunnus* and *Ethynnus* sp.). Jacks tend to travel in large schools and to be semi-pelagic, inhabiting coastal waters and visiting reefs, while the larger tuna commonly live in the deeper waters of the region. Bream (*Sparidae*) and mullets (*Mugilidae*) were important at Shimal as well. In conclusion, the vast majority of the fish eaten at ancient Shimal may be characterised as 'reef-associated pelagics', a clear indication that boats were being used to reach the reefs which were located a considerable distance away from the flat and rather muddy coastal waters off the coast of Ras al-Khaimah.

In addition to studying the physical remains of fishbones and mollusc shells, biological anthropologists have been able to document the intake of food coming from the marine environment in their analyses of human skeletal remains. Two types of analysis have been particularly important. Dental anthropologists have shown that the teeth of people living at sites like Umm an-Nar and Tell Abraq show a great deal of attrition. This must have been caused by the inclusion of abrasive elements in the diet, such as the fairly coarse grit typical of bread made from stone-ground flour, the sandy grit in dried fish and the fine, powdery grit contained within shellfish. Trace elements in bone mineral and stable carbon and nitrogen isotope ratios in bone collagen can also be used to demonstrate the consumption of fish by coastal populations. At Shimal, for example, high strontium (Sr) and copper (Cu) values in bone from a tomb of the mid-second millennium have been interpreted as an indication that the marine food-web – more specifically oysters – was heavily relied upon as a protein source.

Sites such as these all reflect the early exploitation of marine resources, but there are important differences between them which should be underscored. In very broad terms, we can see that the aggregate number of species exploited on the coastal sites of the UAE increased through time. Thus, a far greater number of species was exploited at Umm an-Nar than at al-Madar. But there are qualitative differences between the sites of different periods which may have more to do with modes of living than with the technical means of hunting, fishing and shellfish-gathering. The shell middens of al-Madar and nearby Ramlah, for example, may reflect a good deal about the specific activity of shellfish gathering and exploitation, but they may not, in fact, be representative of sites characterised by what could be called 'communal living'. Similarly, the dugong-butchering site of Akab seems to be a highly specialised 'work station' or 'activity area' rather than a fully functioning early village settlement. Why is this significant?

Dugong bones from an ancient fishing camp.

Sites such as Akab and al-Madar probably reflect but one facet of a community's subsistence strategy in action. The fact that traces of other activities, such as stone tool manufacture, shell ring production, copper casting for the manufacture of fishhooks, cooking, etc. are absent strongly suggests that these were specialised sites of very restricted scope rather than the fully functional villages of fishing and shellfish-gathering communities. On the other hand, did such an ideal village type ever exist along the coast at this early date? Perhaps all sites were,

The Waves of Time

in some measure, function-specific. Perhaps the notion of a fully integrated village community, borrowed from the agricultural settlements of contemporary Neolithic farmers, is inappropriate for the understanding of early coastal occupation in the UAE. Fishing, after all, took place directly on the beach, perhaps in boats of limited capacity and sailing potential. Fish drying may have occurred close to the very spot where the catch was hauled in. Shellfish gathering took place in different lagoonal areas, near rocky inter-tidal beds. Shellfish may have been opened close to where they were gathered in order to avoid the necessity of hauling heavy baskets or sacks of oysters to the actual encampments of the coastal inhabitants. Actual habitation sites, probably no more substantial than a series of palm-frond houses or *barastis* behind a fossil sand dune (situated so as to be out of the winter wind or *shamal*), would have left behind them few traces other than areas of burning where fires were lit, a thin scatter of debris, and postholes now virtually undetectable in the sand.

The settlements on Umm an-Nar, at Tell Abraq, and at Shimal, however, differed from al-Madar or Akab in that they have each yielded a wide range of remains coming from wild, hunted terrestrial fauna (e.g. gazelle, oryx and camel), domesticated animals (sheep and goat), fish, grinding stones, casting spillage from the manufacture of copper objects and so on, as well as houses constructed from slabs of beach rock or *farush* (e.g. at Umm an-Nar), palm-fronds (Tell Abraq), or locally available rock at the base of the mountains (Shimal). Umm an-Nar has all the hallmarks of an early village, but it should not be used as a benchmark against which all other coastal sites are to be measured. With a large, circular fortress surrounded by *barasti* houses, Tell Abraq's lay-out is completely different, while the houses at Shimal, almost certainly constructed from a combination of stone and thatch or matting, represent yet another adaptation to the coastal environment which clearly reflects the different sorts of building materials available in the far north of the country.

One further remark may be made about the presence of sheep and goat on coastal sites. Since neither the sheep nor the goat was independently domesticated in eastern Arabia, each must therefore have been introduced by the earliest colonists who came to the region c. 5000 BC. Faced with the riches of the sea, what need could early coastal dwellers have had of sheep and goat? The answer to this is surely not protein. Fish and shellfish provided a more than ample source of protein for the early coastal population. Rather, sheep and goat fulfilled two important functions. They provided fleece and hair which could be used to make cloth; more vitally, sheep and goat turned brackish water unsuitable for human consumption into drinkable milk which could be consumed either directly or made into yoghurt and cheese. Historic sources from the recent past are full of comments on the brackish nature of the water along the Gulf coast of the UAE. The traditional import of sweet water by boat from wells on the western island of Dalma to Abu Dhabi, and the transport of well-water by donkey and camel from Falaj al-Mualla to the town of Umm al-Qaiwain are but two cases illustrating the provision of drinking water on the coast from relatively distant sources. Sheep and goat are, quite literally, 'walking water purification systems', and would have been far more valued for this than for their meat in ancient east Arabia.

Decorative uses of shell and fishbone

Up to this point the discussion of marine resources has focused largely on fish, shellfish and crustaceans which were caught or gathered in order to be eaten. But there are other important and often symbolic associations between humankind and the sea which we can already observe in remote antiquity.

One of the most remarkable aspects of beads and pendants in antiquity was the almost universal belief in their magical and protective powers. Different types of stones and their colours were associated with different prophylactic abilities, as early Arabic literature amply attests. It is intriguing to find therefore, that prehistoric sites in the UAE have yielded literally thousands of beads made of shells and small fish vertebrae, and it is difficult to believe that this is not a reflection of a belief system in which protection from harm at sea, propitiation of deities associated with the sea and perhaps prayers for an abundant yield from the sea all played a role. On the other hand, fashion and exoticism may also have contributed to the distribution of shell beads on sites throughout the UAE for it is striking that the third millennium tomb at al-Sufouh in Dubai, which is located close to the coast, yielded only 30 dentalium or 'tusk shell' beads (*Dentalium octangulatum*), whereas an inland site like Jebel al-Emaleh in Sharjah yielded, in the first season alone, some 223

beads of various shell varieties. These included 128 examples of *Conus catus*, including a necklace made exclusively of Conus beads strung around the neck of Skeleton 1 in Tomb I; 42 examples of *Dentalium*; 21 examples of *Oliva inflata*; 12 examples of *Engina mendicaria*; 8 examples of *Peribolus arabica* or cowrie, all of which had been cut longitudinally; and the columella of a *Xancus pyrum* shell which had been perforated at both ends to make a long, tubular bead nearly identical to ones found at the fourth millennium site of Aqab in Umm al-Qaiwain, and closely paralleled by finds dating to c. 3000 BC from Tell Gubba in north-eastern Iraq. Finally, small fish vertebrae, pierced through the centre, were used as spacer beads at a number of third millennium sites, including Jebel al-Emaleh, al-Sufouh and Tell Abraq.

Shell beads were fairly numerous in the third millennium tombs at Jabal al-Emaleh in the interior of Sharjah.

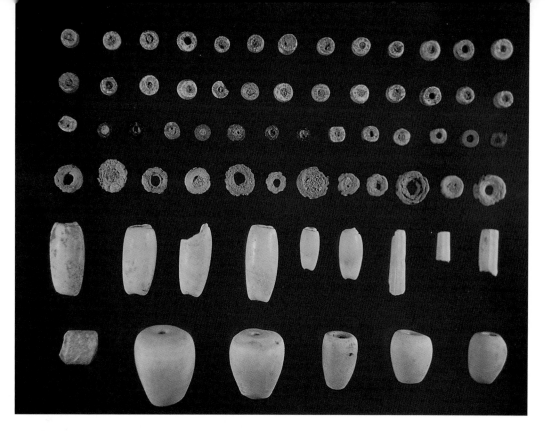

A selection of fish vertebrae and shell beads from the third millennium tombs at Jabal al-Emaleh in the interior of Sharjah.

What is the meaning of the apparently greater number of shell beads on an inland site like Jebel al-Emaleh and their paucity at a coastal site like al-Sufouh? Why are there only 14 shell beads as opposed to roughly 650 stone beads (principally agates, carnelian, lapis or quartz) in the late third millennium tomb at Tell Abraq, another site located close to the ancient shoreline? It can hardly be that the inhabitants of the area around Jebel al-Emaleh were more involved with shellfish and fishing than their counterparts on the coast. Obviously, contact between the coast and the interior, even seasonal migration, may have played a role in effecting the movement of shell from both the Gulf and Arabian Sea coasts to the interior of the country. Was it simply that, located at some distance from the sea, the people of the interior harboured a greater desire than their coastal brethren for the symbols associated with the sea? To wear a necklace made of shell may have meant nothing to a fisherman or shellfish gatherer living on the coast of Abu Dhabi or Ras al-Khaimah, for shells were a part of daily life. On the gravel plains of the interior, in the shadow of the Hajar mountain range, on the other hand, shells may have taken on an exotic aura which made them a highly sought element in the personal jewellery of the third and second millennium BC inhabitants of the region.

The Waves of Time

One particular type of shell known as the 'fig shell' (*Ficus subintermedia* d'Orbigny) is common in third millennium graves throughout the UAE. At Tell Abraq, for example, no fewer than 79 examples were found in the collective tomb dating to c. 2000 BC. The fig shell, which has a bulbous, rather deep end tapering to a small aperture, has traditionally been used as a natural baby bottle for feeding liquids to infants. Ethnographic exhibits of traditional lifeways in the museums of the UAE show that this was still practised in the very recent, pre-oil past. Clearly the use of feeding shells for infants is a practice of great antiquity. Considering the large numbers of infants found in the prehistoric collective burials of the UAE it is not surprising that feeding shells should have found a prominent place amongst the grave goods interred with the dead. Indeed, the total number of feeding shells from the tomb at Tell Abraq exceeds that of the ceramic vessels found there.

Two 'feeding shells' (Ficus subintermedia) from the late third millennium tomb at Tell Abraq. Comparable examples are known from many tombs in the UAE.

During the Iron Age, shell was used to make large medallions or buttons like these from a tomb at Sharm in Fujairah. The carved rosette was probably inlaid with a perishable material such as paste or a precious stone.

Finally, during the Iron Age large shell 'buttons' or medallions, some of which were made from the sawn ends of *Conus* shells, were manufactured as decorative items. These are habitually convex with one flat side and generally measure c. 4–5 centimetres in diameter. The upper, convex face is normally decorated with a concentric pattern of double dotted circles and simple circular impressions. Over a dozen examples are now known from such sites as Bithnah, Dibba and Sharm, in Fujairah; Shimal in Ras al-Khaimah; Qarn Bint Saud on the outskirts of Al-Ain; and al-Qusais in Dubai. Comparable finds have been discovered at the Assyrian capital Nimrud in contexts datable to the ninth and eighth centuries BC.

Of dugongs and pearls

Two further raw materials from the marine environment deserve special mention. The first is dugong tusk which, in its density and consistency if not dimensions, provides a suitable substitute for elephant ivory. Three dugong tusk fragments were recovered in the settlement at Umm an-

Nar, and several pieces have been found at Tell Abraq as well. This would certainly have been used to fashion beads, pendants and rings by the ancient inhabitants of the UAE.

Current opinion on the origins of pearling would date the beginnings of this influential activity to the fifth or fourth millennium BC. Interaction between Ubaid-period Mesopotamian visitors and local hosts is indicated by the painted pottery of so-called Ubaid type which has been picked up on an increasing number of sites from Dalma, in the far west, to Ras al-Khaimah, in the north-east. Such interaction is generally believed to have involved an exchange of goods. Obviously, the most tangible evidence of the Mesopotamian presence is undoubtedly the distinctive painted pottery of Ubaid type. But what could the ancient inhabitants of the UAE have offered in exchange? Dried fish is a possibility, but it would have been neither exotic nor a staple lacking in the inland and offshore waters of Mesopotamia itself. Copper from the Hajar mountains is a possibility, but there is no evidence for copper mining or use of any kind in south-eastern Arabia at this early date, and most of the early Mesopotamian copper artefacts analysed to date appear to have been made of copper from either the Iranian Plateau or the Zagros-Taurus mountain belt. Yet there is another local resource for which Abu Dhabi and Bahrain were later to become famous, namely the pearl, and scholars have recently suggested that pearls, rather than copper or fish, may have been the motivation behind Mesopotamia's earliest contacts with the Gulf coast of the UAE.

Because of the fact that pearls decompose relatively rapidly, direct evidence of pearling is scarce in the archaeological record. Yet over the years, pearls have been founded singly or in small numbers at several archaeological sites in the UAE, including the fifth or early fourth millennium shell middens and associated burials of Umm al-Qaiwain, where an unperforated example was unearthed; the roughly contemporary cemetery at Jebel Buhays in the interior of Sharjah, which has yielded a perforated pearl; the second and early first millennium BC site of al-Qusais in Dubai; and the sprawling first century AD emporium of ed-Dur between Umm al-Qaiwain and Ras al-Khaimah (see Chapter 2). Certainly the fact that perforated pearls have now been recovered both at Jebel Buhays and in a contemporary, fourth millennium BC cemetery at Ras al-Hamra in Oman supports the contention that they were already an important item in the late prehistoric era.

The mangrove and its importance

Because of the richness of its resource base, particular mention should be made of the inter-tidal zone. This was and is the breeding grounds for a variety of fauna, including virtually all of the shellfish utilised in antiquity, as well as certain species of crustaceans and fish. The tidal flats of the Gulf coast are characterised by pockets of mangrove which, as we know from written sources, were far more extensive in the past than they are today. Mangrove is an important source of both fuel and wood for building purposes. A study of the charcoal from the late third millennium levels at Tell Abraq on the border of Sharjah and Umm al-Qaiwain has documented the presence of two types of mangrove in the region at that time, *Rhizophora* sp. and *Avicennia marina*. Of the two, only *Avicennia* still inhabits the UAE coast, but how and why *Rhizophora* became extinct remains a mystery. Tell Abraq is one of the few prehistoric settlements on the coast of the UAE which has occupation levels dating *In ancient times* from the third, second and first millennia BC and in all of these the bulk *mangroves fringed* of the physical evidence of housing consists of the postholes left by *most of the* UAE the wooden uprights of traditional *barasti* or 'arish houses. While Christ's *coastline.* thorn (*Ziziphus spina-christi*) and tamarisk (*Tamarix* sp.) wood could have been used for house construction, mangrove would also have been available. In later historic times, according to the Greek natural scientist Theophrastus (quoting Eratosthenes), mangrove was used for boat building in the Gulf (on Bahrain) and there is no reason why the same should not have been the case during this much earlier period.

Early coastal cruising, open water sailing and early fishing technology

If it is true to say that the earliest colonists of the UAE coast reached their ultimate homeland by land, it is equally true that they were soon venturing out onto the sea. This is clearly shown by some of the sorts of fish which were being exploited in antiquity, such as jacks, tuna or sea bream (e.g. at Tell Abraq and Shimal). The presence of pelagic species on coastal archaeological sites therefore implies an ability to contend with the sea, as does the recovery of pearls. However, we should be careful not to jump to the conclusion that the human exploitation of deep sea species in the remote past implies the construction of sea-

going watercraft. In the nineteenth century Omani fishermen near Ras al-Hadd were observed by Surgeon H.J. Carter of the Bombay Marine's *Palinurus* to dive into the water with inflated goatskins and to swim out to sea equipped with fishhooks and lines. These men were thus able to fish in deep water without so much as a raft, let alone a boat, at their disposal.

As noted earlier, fish net sinkers are attested on prehistoric sites like al-Madar by the fifth millennium BC. The earliest ones were cobblestones, probably pebbles picked up in the inland wadis of the UAE and brought to the coast where they were often modified by being given a slight 'waist' so that cord, possibly palm-frond twine, could be tied around them. During the third millennium, however, perforated net sinkers appear. These were generally circular, roughly shaped 'doughnuts' of locally available limestone with a perforation made from either side. The net sinkers found in the settlement on Umm an-Nar were generally 10 centimetres in diameter and 2–3 centimetres thick, but their weight varied from under 50 to more than 700 grams, though the majority weighed between 100 and 200 grams. Similar weights are known from Ghanadha and Tell Abraq.

In antiquity net fishing on the coast of the UAE was certainly complemented by line fishing. The settlements of both Umm an-Nar and Tell Abraq have each yielded a small number of both copper and bronze fishhooks, while a small socketed spearhead with an unusually shaped blade from the surface of Umm an-Nar has been interpreted as a fish spear.

Maritime contacts with distant regions

Contact between the ancient coastal population of the UAE and early Ubaid seafarers from Mesopotamia initiated a pattern of long-distance contact with the region's neighbours, both near and far, which has continued unabated to the present day. A thousand years later, around 3000 BC, Mesopotamians bearing painted pottery of so-called Jamdat Nasr type came to the region again, most probably looking for a supplier of copper. Distinctively shaped, Jamdat Nasr vessels are known from a number of so-called Hafit-type graves excavated near the eponymous site of Jebel Hafit near Al-Ain and from tombs excavated further north at Jebel al-Emaleh in the region south of Dhaid. By the middle of the third millennium BC large storage jars of Sumerian type,

A copper fishhook from the second millennium levels at Tell Abraq.

possibly containing oil, were appearing at the coastal site of Umm an-Nar. These vessels have identical counterparts at the sites of Ur and Tell al-'Ubaid in southern Iraq, both key settlements of ancient Sumer. In the centuries which followed, contact was especially intense with the south-eastern corner of Iran, and a distinctively decorated, black-painted grey pottery, best known from such sites as Bampur, Khurab and Damin, found its way to coastal sites in the UAE such as Umm an-Nar, al-Sufouh and Tell Abraq. Closer to 2200 BC imports from the Indus Valley began to arrive in the Gulf region. Once again, coastal sites like Tell Abraq have yielded fragments of distinctive, black-washed storage jars as well as small, cubical stone weights identical to those found at the great cities of the Harappan civilisation, including Mohenjo-Daro, Chanhu-Daro and Harappa itself, all located near the Indus River in what is today Pakistan. Examples of etched carnelian beads, a typical product of the Harappan civilisation, are known from several sites in the UAE including Umm an-Nar (Abu Dhabi), Hili tomb B (Al-Ain), Qattarah (Al-Ain), Dhayah (Ras al-Khaimah), al-Sufouh (Dubai) and Tell Abraq (Sharjah), while flat gold disk beads with a raised midrib from Tell Abraq have identical counterparts at Harappan sites such as Mohenjo-Daro in Pakistan and Lothal in India. Similar gold beads are known from the Royal Cemetery at Ur and Tell Asmar in Mesopotamia, and from Altyn Depe in Turkmenistan. Finally, around 2000 BC distinctive examples of pottery and ivory combs bearing decorations known only in the ancient land of Bactria (today northern Afghanistan and southern

Maritime contact brought a wide range of exotic goods to the UAE in the late third millennium, such as this ivory duck mounted on a rectangular rod, found in the tomb at Tell Abraq.

Ivory combs such as this example from Tell Abraq were imported by land and sea from Bactria or the Indus Valley.

Uzbekistan) appeared at Tell Abraq. Pottery of so-called Kaftari type from Fars province in south-western Iran also arrived at Tell Abraq at this time, though it is impossible to say whether goods like these reached the site via intermediaries in south-eastern Iran and/or the Indus Valley. Whether any or all of these finds reached the shores of the UAE via one or more intermediaries, however, they all must have come by sea.

It would be pointless to catalogue the many sorts of artefactual material which attest to the existence of long-distance exchange without deriving the most obvious lesson from that material in terms of maritime history. Quite clearly, the waters of the Arabian Gulf and Arabian Sea were anything but a barrier to contact between the peoples living on either side of them. On the contrary, both bodies of water united those peoples and facilitated trade and traffic much more than the vast land masses which separated Central Asia from the lower Indus Valley, or Mesopotamia from the highlands of eastern Iran. In recent times the towns which dot the shores of the Gulf have been home to an amalgam of Arabs, Persians, Indians, Baluchis and others. More likely than not, the situation was relatively similar in the late prehistoric and early historic era.

Cuneiform sources

While the scattered sherds of Ubaid pottery from Dalma, al-Madar or Jazirat al-Hamra, the handful of Jamdat Nasr pots from Jebel Hafit and Jebel al-Emalah, and the large Mesopotamian storage jars from Umm an-Nar island are all suggestive of maritime trade between the UAE and Mesopotamia between the late fifth and mid-third millennium, sceptics might argue that the vessels and their contents could just as easily have come overland down the east coast of Arabia. The fact that no evidence exists to support such a long-distance terrestrial route ought to point us away from an explanation like this, however, even if it is difficult to disprove outright. Some use of marine transport is certainly suggested by the presence of Ubaid pottery on the island of Dalma, some 35 kilometres offshore. By the third quarter of the third millennium we have more conclusive evidence of a long-distance maritime relationship between the ancient UAE and the great Akkadian empire in southern Mesopotamia, for at about this time the historical records of the latter state speak of campaigns which were directed against the population of the land known in Sumerian as Magan (in Akkadian, Makkan).

The Akkadian empire was the creation of Sargon of Agade, cup-bearer to the king of the holy city of Kish, one of the most important Sumerian cities in southern Mesopotamia. Around 2350 BC Sargon began a series of conquests with the help of the great god Enlil who, as recounted in one of Sargon's own inscriptions, gave the upstart ruler control over both the Upper Sea, i.e. the Mediterranean, and the Lower Sea, i.e. the Arabian Gulf. This is the first time in history that we can put an ancient name to the shallow epi-continental sea which was to play such an important role in the history of the UAE, and from then on the term 'Lower Sea' was the standard designation for the Gulf in most cuneiform records from Mesopotamia. Only once in the period just before 2000 BC was the alternative name 'Sea of Magan' employed.

But there is a second text of Sargon's which is equally important. In it, the Akkadian king boasts that 'ships from Dilmun, Magan and Meluhha docked at the quay of Agade', his capital. We now know conclusively that this trinity of toponyms describes Mesopotamia's three most important southern trading partners: Dilmun – the modern island of Bahrain; Magan – the Oman peninsula; and Meluhha – the Indus Valley or Harappan civilisation. Thus, not only does Sargon put a name to the body of water which fronts six of the seven United Arab Emirates (only Fujairah is bounded solely by the Gulf of Oman or Arabian Sea), but he also gives us the ancient name, in Sumerian, for the landmass now occupied by the UAE and the Sultanate of Oman. Magan makes its first appearance in recorded history, and since Sargon tells us that ships from Magan tied up at the quay of Agade, we can be certain that its ancient inhabitants – the bearers of the archaeological culture named after the island of Umm an-Nar where it was first discovered – were more than adequate seafarers. Even if the precise location of Sargon's capital at Agade remains to be determined, it is generally acknowledged that it must lie somewhere near modern Baghdad in central Iraq. Thus, Sargon tells us that ships from Magan must have been capable of navigating northward through the waters of the Gulf, perhaps via Dilmun (modern Bahrain), and on up the Euphrates. The likelihood of sailing up the Tigris is less strong, although it cannot be absolutely ruled out.

Two of Sargon's successors, his son Manishtusu and his grandson Naram-Sin, are known to have conducted military campaigns against Magan. In the case of Manishtusu, the attack was most definitely a naval one. According to his so-called 'Standard Inscription', Manishtusu had a fleet built in south-western Iran where he had recently concluded campaigns against Anshan and Sherihum; he then crossed the Lower Sea where he encountered a force of some 32 'cities' which had come together to meet him. After subjugating the cities and their lords, Manishtusu marched to the metal mines (presumably the copper mines in the interior of the UAE and/or Oman), quarried black stone in the mountains (presumably diorite), loaded this on his ships and sailed back to Akkad where he had a statue fashioned in honour of Enlil, his divine protector. Not long afterwards Manishtusu's son Naram-Sin was forced to launch a second attack against Magan. After subjugating the country, he captured the king Manium and quarried more black stone which he brought back to Agade like his father.

These passages raise as many questions about Magan as they answer. To begin with, it seems difficult to credit the UAE and Oman with something on the order of 32 'cities' during the late third millennium BC. Yet neither this number nor the designation 'cities' should be viewed as inconsistent with the remains of the Umm an-Nar culture uncovered to date. When the Akkadians used the term 'city' they thereby designated everything from a small village to an urban metropolis, and it is certainly the case that 32 sites of the Umm an-Nar culture can easily be accounted for if we examine the combined archaeological record of both the UAE and Oman. Indeed, one of the main features of the late third millennium throughout the region is the prevalence of settlements with strongly fortified, circular towers, the forerunners of modern towers such as the great fort at Nizwa. Tell Abraq, located directly on the coast of the UAE, boasted a large tower built of mudbrick faced with stone and this is likely to have been one of the settlements captured by the warring king Manishtusu. On the other coast of the UAE a similar fort, though made largely of mudbrick, was built where the village of Bidya now stands.

Yet why would an Akkadian king have set sail from south-western Iran with a flotilla of ships against such a seemingly distant neighbour as Magan? The answer to this lies in a simple word: resources. Manishtusu's reference to the metal mines and the allusion which both he and his son Naram-Sin make to the quarrying of black stone for the fashioning of divine statues reveal a pre-occupation with two of the terrestrial resources of the UAE – copper and metamorphic rock – which have long been utilised by the region's local inhabitants. Other cuneiform sources from approximately the same time refer to the import of copper from Magan to cities such as Ur and Tello in southern Mesopotamia; one speaks of a courier from Magan who was given rations; and soapstone or steatite bowls typical of the UAE, known to have been manufactured by the hundreds and found on virtually all sites, coastal and otherwise, of late third millennium BC date, have been discovered at Tello, Ur and nearby Susa. The likelihood that stone bowls such as these were imported for what they contained, not as trophies of either war or trading expeditions, is strong. The copper of Magan, on the other hand, was a commodity which, prior to the mass exploitation of the great pearl banks off the coast of Abu Dhabi and the discovery of oil, was arguably the UAE's most important exportable natural resource. Abundantly available in the Hajar mountains of the eastern UAE in what is today Ras al-Khaimah, Fujairah and Sharjah territory, Magan copper was greatly in demand at the end of the third millennium BC, although securing its supply was not an easy matter.

The overt hostility of the Akkadian kings towards Magan is clear from their inscriptions and is unlikely to have been conducive to regularised sea trade. Yet one of the city governors who lived after the collapse of the Akkadian empire (c. 2150 BC) apparently tried to establish a less

Early inhabitants used coral rock for building houses and fish traps.

The Waves of Time

belligerent relationship with his southern neighbour. Gudea of Lagash (c. 2100 BC) was governor of one of the most important and ancient southern Mesopotamian cities. Like Bremen and Bremerhaven, or Basra and Fao, Lagash was twinned with its own port of Gu'abba, and carried on a lively maritime trade throughout most of its history down the Shatt al-'Arab and into the Gulf. In one of his many extant inscriptions, Gudea proclaims that his patron deity, Ningirsu, 'opened the way' from the Upper Sea to the Lower Sea, thereby permitting Gudea to acquire those luxury goods – exotic woods, stones and metals – needed for the adornment of Ningirsu's temples. That this was more than a poetic statement is made clear from an economic text dating to the fourteenth year of Gudea's reign which records the disbursement of 241 garments to a merchant bearing the Sumerian name Lugal-inimdu. Without specifying what was meant to be purchased with these textiles, the text simply says that they were 'for Magan'. Interestingly, both wood and diorite were imported into Lagash on Magan ships during the reign of Gudea.

The next major state to rise in southern Mesopotamia after the collapse of the Akkadian empire was the so-called Third Dynasty of Ur. The founder of the dynasty, one Ur-Nammu (c. 2112–2095 BC), proclaims in an inscription found near Ur that he 'restored the Magan trade' (lit. 'boat') to the hands of the moon god Nanna, and in the Law Code of Ur-Nammu we read, 'By the might of Nanna, the lord of the city [of Ur] he returned the Magan-boat of Nanna to the registry [?] place'. A text from the reign of Ur-Nammu's grandson Amar-Sin also contains mention of a disbursement of bread rations to a gang of Magan-shipbuilders.

These allusions to the 'Magan boat' and 'Magan-shipbuilders' raise an interesting issue in the study of early Gulf seacraft. It was very common in Sumerian and Akkadian to qualify nouns with a geographical descriptor. Like Brussels sprouts and China tea phrases such as 'Magan boat' or 'Magan-shipbuilder' contain a specific geographical term which is important, if ambiguous. The ambiguity springs from the fact that we have no way of knowing whether the boat or shipbuilder came from Magan, or whether the terms refer instead to types of watercraft and shipwrights skilled in their construction. In other words, like the Dilmun dates and Magan goats known to have been grown and herded in Mesopotamia, 'Magan boats' may have been a type of boat (cf. the 'Boston Whaler') which was associated with a particular geographical region, no doubt originally because it had been introduced from that

The Waves of Time

area, but which may well have been later built and used in Mesopotamia itself. Perhaps it came to be called a 'Magan boat' because it was the sort of vessel routinely used for sea journeys to that distant land. Indeed the likelihood that this was the case is strengthened by the fact that a text from this period in the British Museum specifies the quantity of bitumen needed 'for caulking Magan boats'. As it happens, the quantity stipulated is a staggering 951,000 litres (c. 475,000 kilograms) but whether this was used to caulk several dozen small to medium-sized boats, or a much smaller number of large, ocean-going craft, is impossible to determine.

The same ambiguity does not, however, surround the topic of Magan copper, for the simple reason that this commodity was completely unavailable in southern Mesopotamia itself. Texts from the reign of Ibbi-Sin (2028–2004 BC), last king of the Third Dynasty of Ur, show us a merchant named Lu-Enlilla engaged in the purchase of Magan copper on behalf of the Nanna temple at Ur. Lu-Enlilla repeatedly took charge of quantities of textiles, hides and jars of sesame oil, as recorded by tablets said to be 'put in a ship for Magan', with which he purchased copper from that country. The mechanics of that trade, at least at the Magan end, are shrouded in mystery, but it is likely that sites such as Tell Abraq, Shimal and al-Sufouh on the coast of the UAE were involved. Umm an-Nar island, on the other hand, was no longer occupied by this late date.

By the early second millennium BC the cuneiform sources mentioning Magan fall silent. That this had more to do with internal political problems in Mesopotamia than with disturbances in the Lower Gulf seems likely, however, for the continued evidence of contact between the UAE coast and Bahrain, Iran and the Indus Valley, so well-illustrated by a range of ceramic and other finds recovered at Tell Abraq, suggests that the silence of the written sources is not indicative of a 'collapse' which can be projected onto the entire region. Goods from these distant lands, each of which was separated from the UAE by water, still reached sites like Tell Abraq, Shimal, Asimah and al-Sufouh, and it is hardly credible to think that the trade was entirely one-sided. But of direct evidence we have little and without the aid of written sources, absent until much later in the UAE, we have no way of confirming the existence of waterborne transport based in Magan, plying the Lower Gulf and Arabian Sea, at this date.

Watercraft of Magan in text and iconography

An Iron Age
pendant from Tell
Abraq with the
earliest depiction
yet discovered of
a ship with
a lateen sail.

As we have seen the Mesopotamian references in cuneiform texts to 'Magan boats' are ambiguous and are as likely to refer to vessels 'in the style of Magan' or those involved in trade with Magan as to ships actually coming *from* Magan. And yet it is clear that the ships of Dilmun, Magan and Meluhha, the three major maritime nations bordering the Lower Sea, were anything but uniform. To ascertain what those seacraft looked like, however, we must turn to archaeological discoveries in the regions themselves, for even if the number of representations of watercraft is small, the differences between them are obvious even to

The Waves of Time

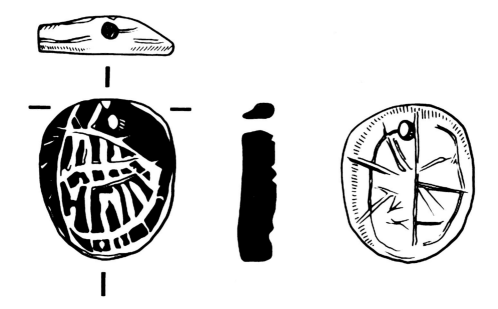

the untutored eye. It is unfortunately true that we lack a corpus of perfectly contemporary representations of watercraft from Bahrain, the Oman peninsula and the Indus Valley, but even allowing for this, a comparison between the extant representations is instructive.

By far the largest number of iconographic representations comes from Bahrain and Failaka (an island off the coast of Kuwait), the twin centres of ancient Dilmun. These are found almost exclusively on stamp seals of so-called 'Dilmun type' which date to the first three centuries of the second millennium BC. Seven Dilmun seals from Failaka and two from Bahrain bear depictions of boats. It is striking that the vessels from Dilmun are all double-ended. Those from Failaka have a raised bow and angular stern, while those from Bahrain have an identically raised and curved bow and stern. Although it is perhaps hazardous to guess on the basis of necessarily schematic depictions on stamp seals, these vessels give every indication of having been, for the most part, plank built. No traces of hatching suggest that they could have been boats made of bundled reeds.

This is not always the case in the Indus Valley. A stamp seal, a seal impressed clay 'tablet', and a graffito on a potsherd, all from the great site of Mohenjo-Daro in what is today Pakistan, depict watercraft in use c. 2000 BC. Two of these are very clearly double-ended, reed vessels with a small cabin on the central deck. These are shown with punting poles, presumably their main mode of propulsion, and would most probably have been used on the Indus River, not on the Arabian Sea. The example depicted in the graffito, as well as four terracotta boat model fragments from Lothal in India, are square-sterned vessels with a sharp bow. A perforation through the bow of the boat models has been taken as an attachment for the rigging.

Finally, from Magan we have but a single representation, albeit a highly important one. A small, generally sub-rectangular steatite pendant from Tell Abraq (26 x 23 x 6 millimetres) dating to the Iron Age (c. 1300–300 BC) bears on one side an engraved image of a ship with deep, curving hull and triangular sail. The lines along the surface of the hull suggest that it may have been a reed boat, but with a square stern and sharp prow this seems unlikely. In light of the later maritime traditions of the region, and in view of the abundant information available from Mesopotamia for the existence of sewn plank vessels by the third millennium, it is more logical to suggest that the Tell Abraq vessel was a sewn plank boat.

Stitched or sewn plank boats constitute a large and diverse body of watercraft attested in northern Europe, the Mediterranean, the Indian Ocean, South Asia and Southeast Asia. Many accounts of sewn vessels have come down to us in Western literature, beginning with that of the anonymous Alexandrian Greek author of the *Periplus of the Erythraean Sea* who, writing c. 60–75 AD, commented on 'boats sewed together . . . known as *madarata*' which were in use in Arabia at that time. The sixth century historian Procopius described the seacraft of the Red Sea and India by saying, 'Nor indeed are the planks fastened together by iron nails going through and through, but they are bound together with a kind of cording' (*On the Persian War* I xix 23–24). Marco Polo, too, has left us a description of the manufacture of coconut palm-fibre rope by the natives of Hormuz during the thirteenth century, noting 'and from that they spin twine, and with this stitch the planks of the ship together'. Less well known is the fact that sewn plank watercraft were already being manufactured in southern Mesopotamia by the late third millennium BC, as texts calling for tons of palm-fibre and palm-leaf rope attest. One document from the Third Dynasty of Ur even refers to 11,787 pieces of wood, specifying which parts of the vessel they were to be used for. Clearly, in view of this evidence, it is entirely possible to conceive of sewn plank vessels in use in the Lower Gulf, as suggested by the Tell Abraq pendant, by c. 1000 BC.

More importantly, however, the single sail on the pendant is shaped like an elongated, roughly isosceles triangle, the point of which ends at the bow of the ship. This is, indeed, a depiction of a lateen or settee sail. The origins and ancestry of the lateen sail have been widely discussed by marine historians. Although it has been widely acknowledged that the Arabs have been using the lateen sail since the beginning of Islam, its eventual diffusion to the Mediterranean and India, where it supplanted earlier square-rigged sails, are topics on which there has been a great deal of speculation and very little new data during the past century. The representation of a lateen sail on an archaeological find from the UAE dating to the Iron Age is therefore little short of revolutionary in terms of maritime history.

We can see from even this limited selection of documents that the seacraft of Dilmun, Magan and Meluhha differed in many important ways from each other, and it is clear from depictions of vessels on Mesopotamian cylinder seals or Egyptian rock engravings that those of the UAE's more distant neighbours were equally distinctive. Local traditions in each of these regions, combined with the availability of building materials and environmental exigencies were undoubtedly responsible for the distinctive character of the seacraft of Magan in antiquity. Moreover, caulking methods probably varied from area to area. All in all, we should expect that, as more research is done into the early seacraft of the Arabian Gulf, greater diversity will emerge and a more nuanced picture of ancient maritime technology will gradually come into focus.

The Assyrians and Persians

In the early part of the second millennium BC a new power known as Assyria emerged in northern Mesopotamia. After exerting considerable influence in the nineteenth and eighteenth centuries BC, Assyria went into decline, troubled by conflicts with the Hittites, Elamites and Babylonians. A brief renaissance in the thirteenth century proved shortlived, but early in the ninth century Assyria began again to grow in strength, emerging as the dominant power in Western Asia during the eighth and seventh centuries BC. Royal Assyrian inscriptions from Nineveh give us a good deal of information on Assyria's campaigns against the Arabs of the north Arabian desert oases such as Adummatu, early Islamic Dumat al-Jandal and modern Jawf in the middle of the Great Nafud in what is today Saudi Arabia, but the evidence relating to the peoples of the Gulf is equally interesting. In 640 BC the Assyrian monarch Assurbanipal received

> *Pade, king of Qade, who dwelt in the city of Izke, [of which of old (?)] no ki[ng] had trodden the boundary of Assyria: by the command of Assur and Ninlil their envoy for good[will] and peace', with their rich tribute, travelled a journey of six months, coming to [my] presence . . .*

Although this text contains no mention of Magan, it in fact refers to the same region. For if we look at the slightly later Old Persian inscriptions from Persepolis we find that Qade was the Akkadian name used at this time for the region known in Old Persian as Maka, itself a cognate of Akkadian Magan. Significantly, Pade's capital Izke can be confidently identified with the inner Omani oasis town of Izki.

This text, which comes from the Ishtar temple at Nineveh, gives us no indication of how Pade reached Nineveh, but it is virtually certain that he must have sailed from the UAE coast up through the Gulf, perhaps stopping off in Dilmun (Bahrain), before proceeding on to southern Iraq (Babylonia) and thence up the Tigris to Assyria. And while the Assyrian king may have swept down on many a fold in his time, there is never any hint of belligerence against the kings of Dilmun or Qade in the texts which have come down to us. Campaigns there were by the dozen against other neighbours, the Arabs of Adummatu included, but no hostilities are ever recorded against the regions of the Lower Gulf.

A different relationship obtained somewhat later between the people of Qade or Maka, as the Persians called it, and the Achaemenid Persian empire. We have no idea whether the region came under Persian control during the reign of the empire's founder, Cyrus the Great, or his son Cambyses, but by the time Darius I (521–486 BC) had dealt with the many rebellions which threatened to undermine his rule, Maka had been annexed as a royal Achaemenid province. Texts written in Elamite, the local vernacular, from the fortification at Persepolis record the disbursement of rations for the satraps of Maka (or Makkash in Elamite), several of whom are attested in the sources and all of whom had Persian names, a fact which suggests they were ethnic Persian governors imposed on the region's indigenous Arabian population. Messengers went back

The Waves of Time

and forth between Maka and the capital Persepolis, located near modern Shiraz, and Susa, near modern Ahwaz, in south-western Iran, and this necessarily entailed sailing across the Gulf, probably from a point on the UAE coast, up to the area of modern Bushire if Persepolis were the destination, at which an ancient land route to Persepolis begins, or alternatively straight up to the Shatt al-Arab and Karun river at the head of the Gulf. We know, however, that this traffic was not entirely one-sided, and that travellers went from Maka to Iran as well as going from

Iron Age chlorite bowl excavated at al-Buhays.

Iran to Maka. One text, for example, is an account of flour rations which were given to a group of travellers from Maka who were described in Elamite as *har-ba-a-be*, a cognate of Old Persian *arabaya*, i.e. Arabs.

These inhabitants of Maka were loyal subjects of Darius. Herodotus tells us that, along with the other inhabitants of the 'Erythraean Sea', a Greek term used for the Arabian Gulf, Red Sea and Indian Ocean generally, they formed part of the XIVth satrapy of the Persian empire. The distinctiveness of the ancient inhabitants of Maka, known in the Old Persian sources as Maciya, is apparent in both ancient literary and iconographic sources. Herodotus, for example, describes their dress, saying that they were 'equipped like the Pactyans' [who belonged to the XIIIth satrapy and were neighbours of the Armenians, living somewhere close to the Black Sea], who 'wore cloaks of skin, and carried the bow of their country and the dagger'. In fact, the dagger in question is almost certainly the short sword of the Iron Age culture of Oman and the UAE, abundantly represented by finds from many sites including al-Qusais (Dubai), Qidfa (Fujairah) and Rumeilah (Abu Dhabi). We can see both the Maciyan dagger, and the dress in question, on the base of the throne of Darius II on his grave relief at Persepolis. The throne is supported by the subject peoples of Darius, and the Maciya is shown wearing only a kilt or short wrap-around skirt which comes to just above the knees, with his short sword suspended by a strap slung over his shoulder.

In 480 BC, during the reign of Xerxes, soldiers from Maka fought at the battle of Doriscus in Thrace, today a portion of north-eastern Greece. With a province located across the Gulf from the imperial capitals of Susa and Persepolis, the Persians must have instituted regular sea transport between the two sides of the Gulf. It is intriguing to think of the ancient predecessors of the coastal population of the UAE making their way to Greece by land and sea 2500 years ago. Like the Australians at Gallipoli, the ancient Maciya probably felt that they were being put into a war in a distant land about which they knew little and cared less. Undoubtedly, however, exposure to the many contingents which made up the army of Xerxes and travel through many and varied landscapes on a variety of land transport and watercraft must have made a profound impression on those Maciyans who made it all the way to Thrace and back. Who knows what innovations in seafaring may have been inspired by experiences such as these, as peoples from all over the Western

Asiatic world were thrown together in the cause of imperial expansion.

When it comes to actual evidence of occupation at this time in the UAE we are less than well-informed about the coastal inhabitants of the Gulf and Arabian Sea. Iron Age sites are by no means abundant along either coast. Shell middens in Sharjah and Hamriyah have been located with the odd Iron Age sherd on top, and considerable Iron Age occupation is attested at Tell Abraq and less so at ed-Dur, in Umm al-Qaiwain, and Shimal and Ghalilah, in Ras al-Khaimah. Slightly inland from Dubai a large number of graves dug into the *sabkha* at al-Qusais have yielded stone vessels and bronze weapons typical of this time period. On the East Coast we have large Iron Age collections of material from a series of re-used second millennium graves at Dibba and Sharm, as well as Iron Age fortifications at Husn Madhab and Awhala, in Fujairah, and Kalba in Sharjah. While these buildings are often set in from the coast it seems clear that, in the case of both Husn Madhab and Awhala, the purpose of the fortifications was to survey and control the adjacent coastal plains and *wadis* leading into the interior. Yet this is not a very large selection of sites and the best evidence of the use of marine resources comes from Tell Abraq with its large inventory of fish, shellfish, marine mammals and crustaceans. Undoubtedly the coasts must have been well-settled, with herding and date-palm cultivation complementing the harvesting of abundant marine resources. Twenty years of searching, however, have identified precious few sites.

In conclusion, the early maritime heritage of the UAE is as rich and varied as the vast array of archaeological finds which pertain to it. Out of the myriad stone tools, fishbones, shells, net sinkers and other paraphernalia of coastal existence we are able to piece together a picture of life on the coasts of the UAE in the remote past. When we add to it the evidence from external sources – cuneiform texts from Ur, Lagash, Nineveh and Persepolis – we begin to get a better idea of how the ancient people of the UAE interacted with their neighbours, and of the exigencies of seaborne transport through time. Twenty years ago it would have been virtually impossible to write a chapter such as this one. Much has changed in that time, as archaeological excavations have been conducted in every one of the seven United Arab Emirates. One thing is certain. If the experience of the past two decades is anything to go by, the years ahead are sure to hold numerous surprises for students of the early maritime history of the UAE.

Seas of Change

Daniel Potts

As we saw in Chapter 1, there is a relatively good record of prehistoric settlement on the Gulf and East coasts of the UAE beginning in the fifth and extending into the second millennium BC. By the Iron Age, however, the evidence begins to thin out. As we move into the later pre-Islamic era (c. 300 BC – 640 AD) the situation becomes even worse. It is scarcely credible to suggest that the coasts were abandoned in favour of the interior, and yet we do not have a single site of the last centuries BC (c. 300–50 BC), on either coast of the UAE.

Far and away the most important site in the UAE of this period is Mleiha, a sprawling agglomeration of domestic settlement areas and individual graves as well as a small square fort located near the village of the same name south of Dhaid in the centre of Sharjah. A less 'maritime' location it is difficult to imagine. And yet excavations at the site have yielded a wide variety of imported goods, ranging from Greek black-glazed pottery and the fragmentary handles of wine amphorae imported from Rhodes to South Arabian beehive-shaped alabaster vessels. Glass produced in the large factories of the Levant and/or Egypt has been found, while several base metal Indian coins point to links

towards the east. Goods such as these obviously entered the country through coastal ports from which they were transhipped overland to the main metropolis of the UAE in the third or second centuries BC. The mechanics of this traffic unfortunately elude us for the few written documents recovered at the site, whether in Aramaic or in the South Arabian alphabet, concern local matters.

If we are to say anything about coastal settlement at this time, therefore, it must be based on external sources. Regrettably, the sources available, principally Greek and Latin, can cause much confusion while doing little to throw light on the period in question. The earliest material available derives from the voyage of Nearchus, the Cretan admiral in whom Alexander the Great vested command over the fleet which in 325 BC sailed from the mouth of the Indus to Susa in Iran at the conclusion of Alexander's eastern campaigns. According to Arrian, one of the principal Alexander historians, Nearchus

> had not been sent to navigate the Ocean, but to
> reconnoitre the coast lying on the Ocean, and the
> inhabitants of the coast, and its anchorages, and its
> water supplies, and the manners and customs of the
> inhabitants, and what part of the coast was good for
> growing produce and what part was bad (Anabasis
> 7.20.9–10).

Sadly, few of the data gathered by Nearchus have survived, although Nearchus himself is cited by such later writers as Theophrastus (372/1 or 371/0–288/7 or 287/6 BC), Aristotle's associate and successor; the geographer Strabo (c. 64 BC– +AD 21); and Juba of Mauretania (c. 46 BC–AD 23), while works attributed to his pilot Onesicritus and fellow seaman Orthagoras were excerpted in antiquity as well.

If the wide array of reports commissioned by Alexander were still extant we would have a vast quantity of material from the late fourth century. Instead, we have nothing but a few anecdotes, not all of which are reliable. Thus, for example, Arrian records the fact that, while cruising along the Iranian shore near the Straits of Hormuz, Nearchus sighted a promontory to the west which he called 'Maketa'. Eratosthenes (c. 285–194 BC), the founder of systematic geography, was quoted by Strabo as saying that the Straits of Hormuz were 'so narrow that from Harmozi, the promontory of Karmania (cf. Kerman), one can see the promontory at Macae in Arabia' and this intelligence was surely drawn from Nearchus as well. The connection between Maketa, Macae and Maka is obvious and generations of scholars have not hesitated to identify Maketa and Macae with the northernmost extension of the Musandam peninsula.

Although Onesicritus, with whom he was often in conflict, urged Nearchus to cross over to the Arabian side of the Straits of Hormuz, presumably to fulfil those commands given by Alexander, the Cretan refused. And yet Nearchus, according to Arrian, did not hesitate to assert

The Waves of Time

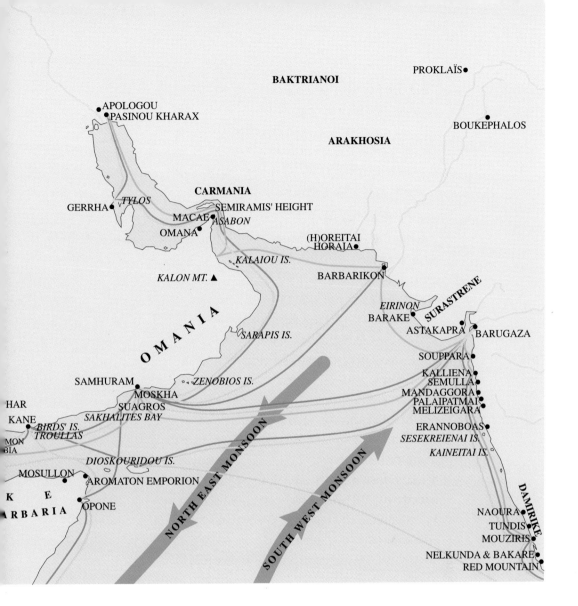

Map of Arabian region as known to the Greeks and Romans.

that cinnamon and other costly Arabian spices were shipped to Assyria from Maketa. The likelihood of this ever having taken place is slim at best, particularly given the paucity of ancient settlement in the generally inhospitable inlets and mountains of Ras Musandam. Furthermore, there is certainly some confusion between the term *mace*, the name given to the covering of the nutmeg, and Maketa, Maceta or Macae, just as later Europeans were to believe mistakenly that nutmeg, known in German as *Muskatnuss*, grew in the hills behind Muscat in Oman!

Thus, when the great Scottish historian W.W. Tarn proclaimed that 'the entire south-eastern part of Arabia was unknown to the Greek world . . . prior to the first century BC' he was closer to the truth than the handful of literary allusions in Greek sources might suggest. We must await Pliny the Elder's *Natural History*, completed in AD 77, before we have more concrete information on the Gulf coast of the UAE, for it is unfortunately the case that none of the three expeditions sent out from Babylonia by Alexander prior to his death in 323 BC produced any intelligence on the Gulf below Bahrain. Nor did Alexander's successors in Mesopotamia, known as the Seleucids after their first ruler, Seleucus I, contribute anything to our store of knowledge about the region. It has sometimes been thought that a Seleucid navy was stationed in the Gulf, but even if this had been the case the only clear evidence of Seleucid naval activity concerns Gerrha, in north-eastern Arabia, and Tylus, the Latin name for the island of Bahrain, for Polybius says that Antiochus III visited both places by ship at the end of the third century BC.

One very murky passage in Pliny's *Natural History* (VI 152) describes a naval battle fought by one Numenius, governor of Mesene (southernmost Iraq), against the 'Persians' at a place called the 'promontory of the Naumachaei' (*Naumachorum promontorium*) opposite the coast of Karmania, i.e. Kerman. Leaving aside the precise date and circumstances of this engagement – the text says that Numenius had been made governor by a Seleucid king named Antiochus, neglecting to specify which one (in fact there were no fewer than eight Seleucid kings by this name) – some scholars have sought to link Naumachaei with Macae and Maketa by emending the text to read 'Machaeorum'. This is highly speculative and one is inclined to scepticism, given that the Latin word for a mock naval battle, *naumachia*, is suspiciously close to the name Naumachaei or Naumachorum.

Quite apart from the few reliable details on the Lower Gulf which they give us, Seleucid and later sources also show a convincing degree of ambiguity in naming the Gulf which is reminiscent of the modern alternatives used variably in scholarly and popular literature. Thus, Theophrastus tended to use the term 'Erythraean Sea' (*Erythra thalatta*), a name which could be applied to the Gulf, the Red Sea and the Indian Ocean in general. Theophrastus also used the term 'Arabian Gulf' (*Arabikos kolpos*) in referring to the Gulf, but later writers normally used the Latin form (*Arabicus sinus*) of this name to denote the Red Sea. Strabo and Arrian, on the other hand, both used the term 'Persian Gulf' (*Persikos kolpos*), as did later Roman historians (*Persicus sinus*), when speaking of the body of water which separates Iran from the Arabian peninsula.

Ed-Dur and the Characene corridor

c. 50 BC – AD 100

Although the total number of coastal sites from the following period is just as small as that from the preceding one, we now have more evidence of occupation along the coast. Small quantities of locally manufactured pottery dating to this period have been picked up on the island of Qarnein, c. 130 kilometres north-west of Abu Dhabi, while second millennium graves on the East Coast, at both Dibba and Sharm, have yielded imported glazed ceramics, probably from Mesopotamia or south-western Iran, showing that tombs such as these were routinely re-used by the later inhabitants of the coastal region. But none of these sites can compare with ed-Dur in the Emirate of Umm al-Qaiwain. The vast site of ed-Dur, which extends over an area measuring c. 1 x 4 kilometres, is dotted with the remains of private houses, both large and small, and graves, single and collective, all of which are made of beach rock or *farush*. In addition, a number of buildings have been excavated which are roughly square or rectangular with round corner towers, suggesting that these were either élite residences or small, fortified manor houses.

A perforated stone like this is still used by fishermen off the coast of Umm al-Qaiwain as a fish net sinker.

Farush is an ideal building material since it forms in the shallow, offshore lagoon system opposite ed-Dur in horizontal slabs. A conglomerate of decomposing shell and sediment, *farush* can be easily broken into flat slabs of varying thickness depending on how deep a given *farush* deposit may be. The houses, public buildings and graves of ed-Dur, like their much earlier counterparts on Umm an-Nar island in the third millennium, show that *farush* was yet another marine resource which was 'harvested' and put to good use in the ancient building industry.

Moreover, although *farush* blocks are naturally very rough, even when shaped into rectangular blocks, they are not unlike modern cement blocks in their capacity to hold a plaster finish. Some of the more élite buildings at ed-Dur such as the larger private houses, the monumental graves and the temple to the Arabian sun god Shams, were all plastered with a fine white lime plaster which disguised the rough texture of the *farush* building blocks and could be made to imitate finely dressed and pecked limestone ashlar masonry.

Broken pieces of pottery were drilled through and used as fish net sinkers in antiquity. These examples come from the surface of ed-Dur.

The Waves of Time

Ed-Dur is located behind a ridge of dunes which protect it from the open if shallow water of the Khor al-Beidha. In spite of some controversy over the precise height of the sea-level at the time of ed-Dur's occupation, it seems clear that a considerable amount of maritime activity took place at the site. For a start, fish contributed by far the bulk of the protein consumed there, and these included both pelagic (e.g. tuna) and inshore (e.g. mullets, groupers, emperors) species although, in contrast to the earlier periods when fish caught in the nearby offshore lagoons of the Gulf coast were dominant, as at Tell Abraq, the preference at ed-Dur was most definitely for the deep sea, pelagic varieties. The abundance of fishnet sinkers recovered in excavations at ed-Dur leaves little doubt that most fish was netted, and bronze fishhooks, well-attested at the earlier site of Tell Abraq, are conspicuous by their absence. Line fishing, then, seems to have been the exception rather than the rule at ed-Dur and there is no evidence that fish traps, which may have been in use by this date on Failaka in the Bay of Kuwait, were ever employed at the site. On the other hand, a series of perforated rectangular lead weights has been found on the surface of ed-Dur, and these might give some hint that line fishing was indeed practised, even if the fishhooks which were used in conjunction with the lead weights have eluded archaeologists and casual visitors to the site.

Shellfish constituted the second most important source of protein at ed-Dur, but while some 20 species were attested in the faunal inventory, five were of particular importance (*Terebralia palustris*, *Murex kusterianus*, *Pinctada margaritifera*, *Saccostrea cucullata* and *Marcia hiantina*). All of these species are edible and all are attested earlier in the region. Terrestrial fauna, including sheep, goat, cattle and pig, formed part of the diet, and dates are abundantly represented. The importance of the date-palm for providing the shade canopy under which other fruits, vegetables and cereals could be grown, such as melons, apricot, peach, lentils, chick-pea, barley, wheat, millet and alfalfa, all of which are attested elsewhere in the Gulf region by this date, cannot be overstated.

Several pieces of coral were recovered at ed-Dur. These may, of course, be intrusive, little more than fragments gathered up inadvertently in the nets of local fishermen. On the other hand, it is intriguing to recall that in many parts of the world coral has long been known for its allegedly magical and prophylactic properties, and the hanging of a coral pendant around a child's neck is still common in some countries today. Shortly after AD 200 Solinus wrote that, according to Zoroaster, coral had 'a certain power and salubrious effects', while Pliny extolled its sacred and prophylactic characteristics. It has even been suggested that the plant which the Mesopotamian hero Gilgamesh sought to extract from the Lower Sea and which is described as having a 'thorn like that of an *amurdinnu*' was a coral and not, as commonly assumed, a pearl. Moreover, although the Romans may have felt that the best coral came from the Mediterranean, Pliny (*Natural History* XXXII 21) knew of other coral in the Red Sea and it is not impossible that the 'sea producing corals and genuine pearls' of the Chinese sources and mentioned, for example, in the *Wei-lo* or *Abridged History of the Wei Dynasty* by Yü Huan, a text composed sometime between c. AD 264 and 429, refers to the Arabian Gulf.

While the subsistence needs of the ancient inhabitants of ed-Dur were largely met by maritime resources, the sea was important to them in other, more commercial ways. Just as the Silk Road served to link China and the West by land, two maritime routes joined East and West by sea. The more famous of these is the one described in the anonymous mariner's handbook alluded to in Chapter 1 known as the *Periplus of the Erythraean Sea*. This important text, composed sometime around AD 60–75, enumerates the ports on the Egyptian and Somalian coast of the Red Sea, the south coast of Yemen, and the west coast of India. The *Periplus* is a typical mariner's handbook, written in a straightforward, non-literary style of Greek for those literate ships captains who, making full use of the monsoon cycle, brought Indian and other eastern luxury goods including silk and spices from the East to Rome and the Mediterranean world.

But there was another route of equal importance, albeit one which was scarcely mentioned in the Roman sources for it was in the hands of non-Romans. Part of the route is alluded to tangentially in the *Periplus* when reference is made to two ports in the Gulf, Apologos and Omana. Apologos, like the later Islamic harbour at al-Ubulla, lay in southern Iraq and functioned as the main port of call in that region for ships coming up the Gulf. The author of the *Periplus* calls it (§35) 'a market town designated by law . . . situated near Charax Spasini and the river Euphrates'. Omana, located in south-eastern Arabia, was its counterpart in the Lower Gulf and is likely to be the ancient name of ed-Dur. Omana is called 'another market-town of Persia', perhaps suggesting that the Parthians, the dominant power in Iran at this time, exercised juridical and commercial rights there. 'To both of these market-towns large vessels are regularly sent from Barygaza [Bhrigukaccha/Bharukaccha as it was known in early Indian sources, the modern port of Broach situated close to the mouth of the Narmada River on the Gulf of Cambay in India], loaded with copper and sandalwood and timbers of teakwood and logs of blackwood and ebony. To Omana frankincense is also brought from Kana' [modern Bir 'Ali on the coast of Yemen, the seaport for Hadhramawt], the *Periplus* tells us, while 'pearls, but inferior to those of India; purple, clothing after the fashion of the place, wine, a great quantity of dates, gold and slaves' were exported from Omana.

This list of goods is important and at the same time problematic. Pearls were already being utilised in the late prehistoric era. But it was during the Roman era that their importance in the West reached new heights. In his *Natural History* (IX 54–8) Pliny says, 'The first rank, and the very highest position among all valuables belongs to the pearl', albeit those from Sri Lanka (ancient Taprobane) were most highly prized by the Roman clientele. The details of pearl production in the oyster were described by Pliny in the first century AD; by the second century Sophist Athenaeus who refers in his *Deipnosophistai* or *The Sophists at Dinner* to the pearls of 'a certain island in the Persian Gulf' (Bahrain); and again in the third century by Philostratus in his *Life of Apollonius of Tyana* whose description of pearling in the Indian Ocean is followed by a short statement which reads, 'The Arabians of the opposite shore are also said to practise this fishery' (3. 57).

Today, almost 2000 years later, it is difficult for us to conceive just how important pearls were in Rome. Pliny says (*Natural History* IX 117):

Our ladies glory in having pearls suspended from their fingers, or two or three of them dangling from their ears, delighted even with the rattling of the pearls as they knock against each other . . . .I once saw Lollia Paulina [died c. AD 48], the wife of the Emperor Gaius . . . covered with emeralds and pearls, which shone in alternate layers upon her head, in her hair, in her wreaths, in her ears, upon her neck, in her bracelets, and on her fingers, and the value of which amounted in all to 40,000,000 sesterces; indeed she was prepared at once to prove the fact, by showing the receipts and acquittances. Nor were these any presents made by a prodigal potentate, but treasures which had descended to her from her grandfather, and obtained by the spoliation of the provinces. Such are the fruits of plunder and extortion!

Little wonder then that the Romans were so intent on pursuing any trade by which they were able to acquire pearls.

In this regard it is interesting to note that pearling was certainly practised at ed-Dur, as the recovery of a bell-shaped, lead pearl diver's weight, complete with iron ring attachment for a rope, attests. Moreover, stacks of pearl oyster shells were found outside the entrance to one of the monumental graves at the site, suggesting a particular votive practice involving the pearl oyster may have been carried out before the tomb was sealed. It is difficult to believe that the large pearl oyster shells from ed-Dur came all the way from the great pearl bank off the coast of Abu Dhabi, however. More likely than not, large pearl oysters inhabited the waters in the vicinity of ed-Dur when the site was occupied.

Apart from pearls the other goods mentioned in the *Periplus* in association with Omana are equally interesting, for their variety is considerable. Whatever purple dye was sent from Omana is likely to have been imported. Pliny (*Natural History* IX 60–63) says, 'In Asia the best purple is that of Tyre, in Africa that of Meninx and Gaetulia, and in Europe that of Laconia'. The wine mentioned as an export of Omana in the *Periplus* was, if not transhipped foreign wine from the Mediterranean, then almost certainly date wine, while the dates themselves would surely have been local Arabian ones. The gold in question is likely to have been either Roman coin, acquired obviously via trade with the Roman empire, or just possibly Arabian gold, perhaps from the famous mines in western Saudi Arabia at Mahdha Dahab.

The author of the *Periplus*, although aware that ships sailed regularly between Apologos, at the head of the Gulf; Omana, in the Lower Gulf; and Barygaza, in India, neglected to tell his readers and was perhaps himself unaware of the fact that this was but one part of a much more extensive route stretching all the way from the Mediterranean to India. Unlike the Red Sea route described in the *Periplus*, however, the Gulf route was coupled with an overland sector. The western hub of the land route was the great caravan city of Palmyra in the Syrian desert, easily reached from the Mediterranean by three major roads leading to it. Of these, the northernmost led from Antioch down the Orontes river to Epiphania (Hama) where a desert track struck south-east towards Palmyra; a second, east-west route ran from Emesa (Homs) to Palmyra; while a third route ran inland from Damascus and thence north-east via Nazala (Qaryatein). Heading east from Palmyra one could either

Pearl oyster shells were often found at ed-Dur. This large example was one of a whole stack of shells found just outside the entrance to one of the monumental tombs excavated at the site. These had clearly been put there intentionally, perhaps as an offering.

follow the Emessa–Palmyra road all the way to Dura-Europus on the Middle Euphrates, or take a better provisioned caravan route south-east through a series of *caravanserais* which ultimately reached the Euphrates in the vicinity of modern Hit. From here, caravans picked up river barges plying the Euphrates as far as Apologos, where they collected goods which had arrived by sea from Barygaza and Omana, turned around, and began the return journey overland to Palmyra laden with luxury goods. Experience has shown that this was much easier than trying to sail up the Euphrates against the streamflow. What we know of this trade derives principally from inscriptions found at Palmyra which came originally from the bases of statues honouring the leaders of successful caravans (*synodiarchs*) by various trading companies (*archemporoi*). The Palmyrene texts tell us that in addition to Apologos, other market towns in lower Iraq, including Forat, Teredon, Ampa, Digba, Apamea-of-Mesene and Spasinou Charax were all destinations of the overland caravans.

It is important to underscore the fact that while Parthia was generally Rome's greatest neighbour and adversary in the east, with the Euphrates forming the boundary between the two empires for much of their joint history, a small semi-independent kingdom based at Spasinou Charax held the pivotal 'point position' at the juncture of the maritime and overland routes. The history of this kingdom can be told in relatively few words. Founded in 127 BC by an ambitious and rebellious governor named Hyspaosines (hence the name 'Spasinou' Charax) who seized the opportunity to create a new state in the wake of the Parthian conquest of southern Mesopotamia, Charax was both a city and a city-state, becoming the centre of the kingdom of Characene. We have a series of Palmyrene caravan inscriptions dating to between AD 19 and 269 which document the role of the kingdom of Characene as the middleman between the overland and maritime sectors of this alternative to the *Periplus* route. These texts also show us that at least one king of Charax named Meredat succeeded in extending his control down the Gulf; for a text from AD 131 mentions an ethnic Palmyrene who was employed as governor of the *Thilouanoi*, i.e. the inhabitants of Tylos or Bahrain, while a slightly later series of coins issued by Meredat in AD 142 calls him BACILEYC OMAN, or 'king of the Omani'.

A tetradrachm of Attambelos IV, king of Characene, from the surface of ed-Dur. The coin dates to AD 58/9.

It is, therefore, particularly interesting to find that ed-Dur is the only site in the region at which Characene coins have been found. These include a bronze of uncertain attribution, a tetradrachm of Attambelos III (AD 38/9), two tetradrachms of Attambelos IV (AD 58/9) and two tetradrachms of Attambelos VI (AD 104/5 and 105/6). Given its position and clear evidence of contact with the kingdom of Characene, ed-Dur is surely the prime candidate for the site of ancient Omana in the Lower Gulf, a possibility made even more distinct by the wide range of imported luxury goods found there in excavations. Dozens of complete and hundreds of fragmentary vessels of Roman glass have been found at ed-Dur, including pillar-moulded bowls, almond-

bossed beakers, pear-shaped flasks and zoomorphic vessels. Furthermore, a small quantity of Roman *terra sigillata* has also been found at the site. Interestingly, ed-Dur has also yielded a single *aureus* of the Roman emperor Tiberius (Pontif Maxim type), and this is precisely the type of coin which, along with the issues of Augustus, were used by Roman traders involved in the sort of trade described in the *Periplus*.

As far as contacts with other regions go, ed-Dur boasts several sherds of Indian Red Polished Ware and at least one square Indian base metal coin from northern or central India as well as sizeable quantities of black-on-orange Namord ware from south-eastern Iran or Baluchistan. Fine eggshell ware from southern Mesopotamia is also present at the site. Taken all together, the finds from ed-Dur paint a picture of a cosmopolitan centre trading with the far corners of the world, from Syria and Mesopotamia to India. Given the breadth of those contacts, we are justified in asking whether they extended even further, to the very source of the silk so keenly sought in the Roman world?

Roman glass was widely exported in the first century AD. These examples come from a monumental grave at ed-Dur.

This bell-shaped lead weight with iron attachment comes from a first century AD context at ed-Dur. It is the earliest pearl diver's weight known in the Gulf and closely resembles weights used in the nineteenth and twentieth century by pearl divers in the UAE.

Several Chinese sources bear on this question, including Fan Yeh's (AD 420–477) Hou-Han Shu, or the *History of the Former Han Dynasty*, where we read (Vol. 118):

The Roman orient trades with Parthia and India by sea and gets great profit, ten times the capital . . . Their kings always hope to communicate with Han China. But Parthia wishes to trade Chinese silk with Rome, and disturbs the Roman trade with China, and so Rome herself cannot come to China.

If Parthia, by which we may probably understand Charax, was importing Chinese silks by sea via India and re-selling them to Rome, then this description is a clear reflection of the Palmyra–Apologos–Omana–Barygaza trade route through the Gulf outlined above. But the account makes it equally clear that it was in the interest of the Parthians to exclude Rome from direct contact with China, for it threatened her monopoly over the silk routes, both overland and maritime. Indeed, when Pan-chian, governor general of the 'Western Region', i.e. Chinese Turkestan, sent an ambassador named Kan-ying to Rome sometime between AD 32 and 102, the emissary is said to have reached Tiao-zhi, probably Susa or Susiana in south-western Iran, and to have seen the head of the Gulf for himself. Desirous of sailing on to Rome, i.e. down the Gulf, around the bottom of Arabia, and up the Red Sea, he was told:

> The ocean is so vast that if one is lucky he may come back by three months, but if unlucky, it will take for him two years to return. To meet the matter, they had to bring with them food for three years, but many died from homesickness . . .

whereupon Kan-ying abandoned his mission and returned to Chinese Turkestan. A similarly daunting description of sailing from Charax, known in the Chinese sources as Ankucheng, is given in the *Wei-lo*, where we read:

> From Ankucheng in the Parthian territory one may sail westward. If the wind is favourable, he may reach the destination in two months. If the wind is feeble, it will take one year. If no blow of wind, it will take even three years . . . .

It is clear from these accounts, so similar in their dismal description of the prospects for direct sailing to 'Rome' from the Gulf, that the Parthians (and/or Characene merchants) tried their hardest to dissuade the Chinese from even contemplating making direct contact with the Roman markets.

A more ambiguous statement is, however, contained in *Sung-shu* (AD 420–478), where we read:

> As regards Ta-ts'in [Syria] and T'ien-chu [India], far out on the western ocean, we have to say that, although the envoys of the two Han dynasties have experienced the special difficulties of this route, yet traffic in merchandise has been effected, and goods have been sent out to the foreign tribes, the force of the winds driving them far away across the waves of the sea . . . All the precious things of land and water come from there, as well as the gems made of rhinoceros horns and chrysoprase, serpent pearls, and asbestos cloth . . .; also the doctrine of the abstraction of mind in devotion to the lord of the world [Buddha] – all this having caused navigation and trade to be extended to those parts . . .

This statement seems to suggest that, while the envoys described in the Han history may have been rebuffed, the Chinese nevertheless did succeed in establishing direct sea trade with the West. Unfortunately, we cannot say by what date this may have been achieved. Given the lack of anything Chinese at the site, it remains in any case unlikely that Chinese ships were among those which anchored off the coast of ed-Dur in the first century AD.

Pliny's Natural History and Claudius Ptolemy's Geography

Earlier, mention was made of Pliny the Elder's *Natural History* (finished AD 77), a work roughly contemporary with the *Periplus of the Erythraean Sea*. Pliny's work is important, if difficult to use. As the late German scholar Hermann von Wissmann once noted, Pliny's *Natural History* is often confused, jumping from one topic to the next and, in the case of his geographical descriptions, juxtaposing completely unrelated lists of names and descriptions of territory as though they belonged to contiguous regions. It is, von Wissmann felt, as if Pliny had worked with a great number of index cards, and when some of these fell on the floor, he was none too careful in picking them up and restoring them to their rightful place. Thus, although Book VI of the *Natural History* contains a long passage describing south-eastern Arabia, with the names of tribes, towns, ports, islands, mountains, and other physical features, it is notoriously difficult to disentangle what properly belongs there from

Classsical Arabia according to Ptolemy, c. 150 AD.

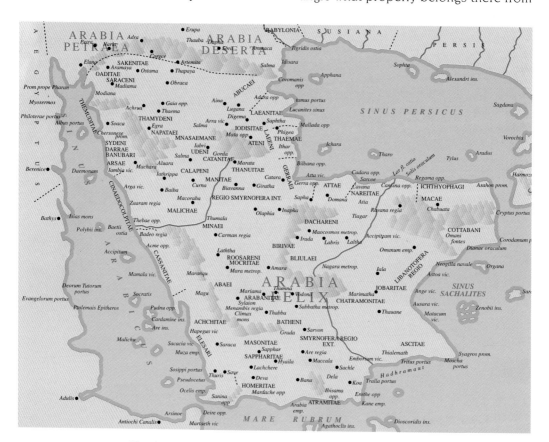

The Waves of Time

what has merely been inserted through mechanical, if unintentional, error. Because virtually none of the names mentioned by Pliny can be identified with any certainty, it is pointless to review them here. One only should be singled out, the *gens Kadaei* or Kadaei tribe, since this seems to represent the same Qade attested as the name for the UAE and Oman in the Neo-Assyrian and Achaemenid sources.

However difficult it may be to make conclusive identifications of the names of peoples and places in south-eastern Arabia recorded by Pliny, they at least show us that the coast of what is today the UAE was well-populated and contained more towns than the solitary discoveries at ed-Dur would suggest. The same can be said of the slightly later (c. AD 150) *Geography* of the Greek geographer Claudius Ptolemy. Once again, it is useless to debate whether or not names such as *Sarkoe polis* can be related to modern toponyms such as Sharjah, or *Kabana polis* to Umm al-Qaiwain, as some scholars suggested in the nineteenth century. Like Pliny's *Natural History*, the main contribution of Ptolemy's *Geography* is to confirm the presence of numerous named sites and groups all along the coast of the UAE during the first centuries of the Christian era.

The Sasanian presence

In AD 224 a prince named Ardashir overthrew the Parthian governor of Fars province in south-western Iran and set about conquering the Parthian empire. In its place was founded a new state of even larger proportions which takes its name from that of one of Ardashir's ancestors, Sasan. The Sasanians did not immediately put an end to the Palmyrene caravan trade with southern Mesopotamia, for the latest caravan inscriptions date to the years AD 247, 257 and 269. But it would not be long before the 'Characene corridor' linking southern Mesopotamia and India via Omana and Apologos was fully in Sasanian hands, and indeed several accounts of the campaigns of Ardashir himself describe a campaign against 'the country of what lies between 'Uman and al-Bahrain and al-Yamamah and Hagar' (*Nihayatu'l-irab fi ahbari'l-furs wa'l-'arab*, c. AD 1000) which would suggest that the UAE was indeed a target of Sasanian aggression by the first years of the new empire's existence. In this regard it is instructive to note the discovery of a tetradrachm of Ardashir on the island of Ghallah in the Umm al-Qaiwain lagoon, although this could have arrived at a later date.

This tetradrachm was minted by Ardashir, founder of the Sasanian empire. It was found on the island of Ghallah in the lagoon of Umm al-Qaiwain.

Were Sasanian soldiers garrisoned in the ancient UAE? This is a possibility raised by a number of sources. Certainly it is widely acknowledged in literary sources that the Sasanian military capital in the interior of the Oman peninsula was at Rustaq in what is today the Sultanate of Oman. Yet in the UAE we have archaeological evidence as well which may shed light on this question. Two individuals, one with an iron long sword and some fragmentary armour, the other with an iron lance, were buried inside two third millennium tombs at the site of Jebel al-Emaleh in the interior of Sharjah. Radiocarbon dates from the graves point, in the first case, to a date of c. AD 628–635 and in the second to a date of c. AD 541–610. Both individuals were mature males, aged 35–39 and 25–30 years, respectively. Do we have here representatives of the class of Sasanian heavy cavalrymen known as *clibanarius* who were noted for their use of the long spear and sword? It is certainly a possibility, and perhaps not irrelevant to note that it was at about this time, in AD 575, that the Sasanian *shahanshah* Khusraw Anoshirwan sent an expeditionary force of some 800 men in eight ships from Iran to Yemen. According to local Omani tradition recorded by Col. S.B. Miles in the late nineteenth century, the Sasanian force embarked from al-Ubulla, ancient Apologos, and stopped at Sohar on the Batinah coast of Oman. Since the Oman peninsula, known in the Sasanian sources as Mazun, had been a Sasanian province since the foundation of the empire, it is quite probable that sea journeys such as this, in which troops were transported back and forth from Iran to Mazun, were a routine occurrence. Certainly ed-Dur, which continued to be occupied into the fourth century AD, has ample evidence of Sasanian glass and pottery, as do several sites in coastal Ras al-Khaimah, including Jazirat al-Hulayla and Kush, while a Sasanian stamp seal was recovered in one of the tombs at Shimal. The small number of numismatic finds made in the UAE, which include the tetradrachm of Ardashir mentioned above, a drachm of Shapur II (AD 309–379) from Ghallah, and a hoard found in Fujairah consisting of late Sasanian coins minted by Hormizd IV (AD 579–590) and Khusraw II (AD 590–628), scarcely give us much indication of the scope of Sasanian political control over south-eastern Arabia at this time, but that control is amply attested by early Arabic, Persian and Armenian historical sources from the first few centuries of Islam.

Fairs in the Pre-Islamic UAE

The late pre-Islamic period saw an abundance of periodic fairs and markets all over the Arabian peninsula, some of which are described in Ibn Habib's *Kitab al-Muhabbar*. Fairs at Dumat al-Gandal, in the Jawf oasis of the Nafud; al-Mushaqqar, in the modern Hofuf oasis of eastern Saudi Arabia; Sohar, on the Batinah coast of Oman; and Shihr, on the Mahrah coast of Yemen, are all described by Ibn Habib. In general, the fairs were held under the protection of a particular tribe or person who acted as guarantor for the safety and well-being of those who visited it, levying a 10 per cent tithe on the goods sold. Other tribes exacted protection money from those travelling to the fairs. Some merchants routinely travelled between these fairs, marketing their wares at different venues according to the season of the year and the climate in any given locale.

Dibba, which is today divided between the Sultanate of Oman and the Emirates of Sharjah and Fujairah, was the scene of one such fair. Ibn Habib calls Dibba

> one of the two ports of the Arabs; merchants from Sind, India, China, people of the East and West came to it. This fair was held on the last day of Ragab. Merchants traded here by bargaining. Al-Julanda b. al-Mustakbir levied the tithe in this fair as in Sohar . . .

This account gives us a number of precious pieces of information. To begin with, it confirms that Dibba was one of the most important harbours and mercantile centres anywhere on the Arabian coast, 'one of the two ports of the Arabs' (the other was Sohar in Oman). Moreover, the text tells us that both Indian and Chinese merchants sailed regularly to Dibba. Obviously, by this date, the Chinese had overcome their fear of the 'Ocean' and were venturing west by sea, not merely relying on the overland Silk Route. Finally, Ibn Habib's account confirms that the fair was in operation during the reign of al-Julanda b. Mustakbir b. Mas'ud b. 'Abd 'Izz who, according to the anonymous Omani chronicle Kashf al-Gumma, died shortly before the embassy of 'Amr b. al-'As, traditionally ascribed to AH 8 (AD 630). Yet we can be sure that fairs such as these had been held for centuries. Writing in the fourth century, the Roman historian Ammianus Marcellinus (AD 330–395) described a fair at Batne, near Zeugma in Roman Syria (by modern Bireçik in what is today part of Turkey), which took place each September and to which many merchants came 'to trade in what the Indians and Seres [Chinese] send, and very many other goods brought thither by land and sea'.

We can thus refute the thesis of the late George F. Hourani according to whom, no direct sailing ever took place between China and south-eastern Arabia in the pre-Islamic era. Certainly by the time Jia Dan (AD 730–805) wrote his *Xin Tang Shu* or *New History of the Tang Dynasty* the maritime route between Canton, Mo-xun (cf. Mazun, the Sasanian name for south-eastern Arabia), and Wu-la (al-Ubulla or Apologos) was well known to Chinese navigators.

Nestorians in the Gulf

The control of south-eastern Arabia by the Sasanians was responsible for more than the movement of goods along the sea lanes. It also accounted for the spread of ideas and religious doctrines. Two religions were particularly prominent amongst the subject peoples of the Sasanian empire, Zoroastrianism and Christianity. Of Zoroastrianism in Arabia we know little apart from the fact that Zoroastrians are referred to on several occasions in texts dealing with the early years of Islam. But on the topic of Christianity we are much better informed.

Aside from some spurious sources such as the *Chronicle of Arbela*, the veracity of which has been called into question by generations of scholars, the earliest reliable work of relevance to early Christianity in the UAE is the *Vita Ionae*, a work describing the life of a monk who flourished in the middle of the fourth century AD. Among other things, this document mentions the existence of a monastery south of Bet Qatraye, i.e. the modern day Eastern Province of Saudi Arabia, 'on the borders of the black island', and for this reason it has been sought by several scholars somewhere amongst the islands of Abu Dhabi. The discovery in 1992 of a Nestorian church and monastery complex at al-Khawr on the island of Sir Bani Yas is therefore of prime significance. Although preserved to only a modest height, the walls of the structures excavated at al-Khawr were finished with fine lime plaster, and discoveries made in the church included decorated relief stucco fragments showing crosses, grape clusters and grape leaves. The church itself is oriented east-west and measures minimally 14 metres from east to west with three aisles. Judging by the ceramics found there the latest phase of the church should be dated to the sixth century AD.

Nestorian church at al-Khawr on the island of Sir Bani Yas.

It stands to reason that getting to and from the island involved sailing, and one might suppose that it was the monastic ideal of seclusion which led Jonah or some other Nestorian monk to found a monastery on an isolated island. And yet isolation was not the normal state of Nestorian monasteries which were, on the contrary, generally integrated into the community, judging by the accounts which have survived of juridical and ecclesiastical matters involving the Church and her members. Thus, we should not assume that an island like Sir Bani Yas was unoccupied when the Nestorian monastery and church at al-Khawr was founded. It is far more likely that a fishing community was already resident on the island. Some slight support for this suggestion may be provided by another important Nestorian document known as the *Chronicle of Seert*. Although composed soon after AD 1036, this text reports on events in the periods AD 250–442 and 484–650. There we read of Abdisho, student of a great proponent of Syrian monasticism called Mar ʿAbda, who is known to have founded numerous monasteries in the reign of the catholicos Tomarsa (AD 363–371). Abdisho, we are told, went to an ʿisland of Yamama and Bahrain', known as Ramath, where he baptised the inhabitants and founded a monastery. Although the island in question is probably to be located further north in the Gulf, perhaps off the coast of Saudi Arabia, the actions of Abdisho suggest that Nestorian monks were not inclined to establish monasteries on unoccupied islands, but rather to minister to what may have been isolated communities some distance from the mainland which were in particular need of pastoral care.

Decorated relief stucco fragment from the Nestorian church on Sir Bani Yas.

Not long before Abdisho's foundation of the Ramath monastery, another proselytiser, the heretical Arian bishop Theophilus Indus, was sent by the Byzantine emperor Constantius on a famous missionary journey. Sometime before AD 344, as we learn from Philostorgius' *Historia Ecclesiastica*, Theophilus set off down the Red Sea for Axum (in Ethiopia) and Himyar (in Yemen). Before returning home he is said to have visited his original home on the island of Dibes/Dibos where he had grown up. This statement has been taken as an indication that Theophilus visited and may have even founded a church at Dibba, and yet nothing could be further from the truth. Scholars have shown that Dibes/Dibos has nothing to do at all with the phonetically similar Dibba, but is instead to be related to Diba/Diva, known in Arabic sources as Dhibat al-Mahal, the name given to the modern Maldive Islands. This is supported by the fact that Theophilus was nicknamed 'Indus', a name unlikely to have been earned by someone associated with Dibba in Arabia!

The real foundation of the Nestorian church can be traced to the important synod of AD 423/4 held at Markabta de Tayyae in Mesopotamia at which the Church asserted its independence from the see of Antioch. Already present at this synod was a bishop from Mazun, one Yohannon, and thenceforth we find the ecclesiastical province of south-eastern Arabia (i.e. the area of the modern UAE and Oman) referred to as Bet Mazunaye. Bishops from Mazun are attested in the acts of the synods of AD 544, 576 and 676.

The sheer distance between the Nestorian communities of the UAE

The Waves of Time

and Oman and the headquarters of the Church at Seleucia-Ctesiphon in Iraq made sea travel up and down the Gulf a necessity if communications were to be maintained. Moreover, judging by the surviving written records, the Churches of Bet Mazunaye and Bet Qatraye seem to have had nearly as much contact, if not more, with the Nestorian Church of Persis, the head of which resided in the town of Rev-Ardashir, near modern Bushire. Early in this century several scholars suggested that with the spread of commerce from southern Mesopotamia in the early Sasanian era the Nestorian Christian message was taken to the far corners of eastern and south-eastern, and this is certainly a possibility. Certainly, the presence in the state of Kerala in south India of six inscriptions in Pahlavi, the script used in the Sasanian empire, on stone crosses strongly suggests a connection with Nestorian Persis. Moreover, one of the Keralite inscriptions reads 'Our lord Messiah may show mercy over Gabriel, son of Chaharbokht. Long life may be for him who made this (cross)'. It is intriguing to note that, in later sources, including both the Persian historian Tabari and the poet Ferdowsi, the name Chaharbokht is explicitly associated with Rev-Ardashir.

The links between Persis and South India perpetuated by Nestorian Christians are part of the same web of contacts which bound the ecclesiastical province of Mazun to Persis and Ctesiphon. It is sobering to consider that none of this contact could have been sustained without constant, vigorous use of the sea lanes that had been in existence since the third millennium BC. Although the *Periplus* may claim that the ability to sail with the monsoon wind was 'discovered' in the first century BC by a Greek named Hippalos, it is obvious from this brief review that mariners plied the route between Mesopotamia, the Lower Gulf, Oman and India from an early date, and continued to do so right into the Islamic era. Indeed, the ocean-going dhows of the present day perpetuate a 5000 year old tradition.

Whether we think of the antiquity of systematic pearl diving, the use of *farush* as a building material, the harvesting of the sea's bounty by fishermen and collectors of shellfish and crustaceans, or the use of shells and fish vertebrae as beads, it is obvious that the ancient peoples of the UAE made full use of the opportunities afforded to them by one of the greatest natural resources available to them. The waters of the Gulf and the Arabian Sea were as familiar to the early inhabitants of the UAE as the mountains and the desert.

Seafaring and Islam

Joseph Elders   BEFORE THE ISLAMIC ERA we hear of Arabia and the Arabs only through the medium of foreigners - Sumerians, Egyptians, Greeks, Romans and Persians - to whom the Arabian peninsula was an exotic, faraway place, frequently of no more than marginal interest to the writer. The situation was to change abruptly with the rise of the Arab nation under the new creed of Islam, and the subsequent rise in status of Arabic to a literary language, a language in which history could be recorded. The Arabs had always been great seafarers, sailing along the maritime trade routes which they now came increasingly to dominate, and many of these travellers and merchants, like Ibn Jubayr, writing in the twelfth century, began to record their experiences. Famous Arab Geographers such as al-Idrisi (twelfth century) charted the sea routes, and skilled navigators compiled books on how to negotiate them, the pinnacle of such endeavour being the works of Ahmed ibn Majid, probably born in the 1430s in the great sea port of Julfar, which is now in the modern Emirate of Ras al-Khaimah.

The information given to us by these great men is supplemented by the writings of the Europeans who penetrated the Indian Ocean, Red Sea and Arabian Gulf in the wake of the Portuguese explorer Vasco da Gama's pioneering voyage to India in 1498, (traditionally, although

erroneously, linked with the name of Ahmed ibn Majid). In addition to these historical sources, a great deal of archeological information has been compiled within the last 40 years with the benefit of modern techniques. Excavations are currently in progress on several sites of the Islamic period, most notably Julfar and Jumeirah, the latter in Dubai Emirate. New information is becoming available almost daily, much of which pertains specifically to the marine heritage of the country, a heritage that, despite the incredible pace of development and change since the discovery of oil, is still very much a living part of the United Arab Emirates today.

The eve of Islam

By the eve of Islam that part of south-eastern Arabia which now forms the UAE had already begun to develop many of the traits which were to characterise the Islamic period. Gulf Arab seafarers and ports had certainly played an important role for at least 3000 years in the trade between the Indian sub-continent and Mesopotamia. The pearling industry, already over 4000 years old, was gaining in importance as a mainstay of the local economy, supplementing trading and fishing as a means of livelihood for the dwellers along the coastal margins of the country. Inland from the coast, a large section of the population continued to live a nomadic lifestyle as they had for centuries. Cultivation and permanent settlements at the oases of Al-Ain, Dhaid and Liwa as well as in the fertile mountainous northern part of the country provided markets and staging posts for the internal trade upon which the bulk of the population depended.

The unification of the Arab world by the forces of Islam had an invigo-
rating and radical effect upon this traditional lifestyle pattern, as Arabia
became the hub of a dynamic and expanding empire from the middle
of the seventh century under the leadership of the Prophet
Mohammed and the Rightly-Guided Caliphs. By the early seventh
century, the Sasanids had succeeded in establishing control by naval
and military power over large sections of the coastline of the Arabian
peninsula, including the Gulf and Batinah coasts of the UAE. There
were Sasanian strongholds and Satraps (Governors) in Bahrain, at ar-
Rustaq and Demetsjerd near Sohar in Oman, and probably also at

The Catalan
Atlas of the Year
1375. 'From the
mouth of the
River of Baldach
[i.e. of Baghdad;
the Tigris] the
Indian and
Persian Oceans
open out. Here
they fish for
pearls which are
supplied to the
town of Baghdad.
Before they dive
to the bottom of
the sea, the pearl
fishers recite
magic spells with
which they
frighten away the
fish' [presumably
sharks].

Dibba and Julfar on the UAE coast. Their power was resented and contested by the local Arab al-Julanda dynasty, who allied themselves with the Muslim forces and, in the year 632, finally managed to expel the Sasanids. Shortly thereafter, the Sasanid Empire was swept away by the Muslim armies.

The archaeological legacy of the Sasanid presence in the UAE is currently coming into focus through the excavations in Ras al-Khaimah of the site of Kush, which is the largest 'tell' (mound composed of human occupation debris, mostly mud-brick) yet found in the Emirates. A large mud-brick fortification has been uncovered there, which can be tentatively identified as Sasanian in date by pottery found in association with it. If Kush is the original site of the ancient port of Julfar, then the area may have been controlled by the Sasanids from this fort on the eve of Islam. Then, as in the Islamic period, control of Gulf trade with its lucrative revenue from the collection of tolls and taxes would have been of critical importance.

The size of the Kush tell and the depth of its occupation layers indicates that even before Islam the site was an important port, with the finding (though only in later contexts thus far) of sherds of Indian red-polished ware dating from the second to fifth century denoting extended trade contacts at this time. The religious beliefs of the inhabitants of pre-Islamic Kush is unclear. There is, however, no evidence of the presence of Zoroastrianism, the state religion of Sasanid Persia, on the Arabian side of the Gulf, and Sasanid influence may have been limited to naval and military control of the coastal margins of the country.

The evangelisation of the Arabian Gulf islands and coastline by Nestorian Christians appears to have followed the maritime trade routes. A Nestorian Christian monastery on Sir Bani Yas island in Abu Dhabi Emirate belonged to either Bet Qatraye or Bet Mazunaye, the two ecclesiastical provinces of south-eastern Arabia. Nestorian missionaries (the so-called St.Thomas Christians), probably passing down the Arabian Gulf, followed the trade routes to India. Some even reached China, as attested by a tablet found in Sian with an inscription in Chinese and Syriac (the ecclesiastical language of the Nestorian church) referring to the foundation of a monastery there in the year 638. Persian and perhaps also Arab merchants in China before Islam thus established the routes for first the Christian, and later the Islamic conversion of sections of the population there.

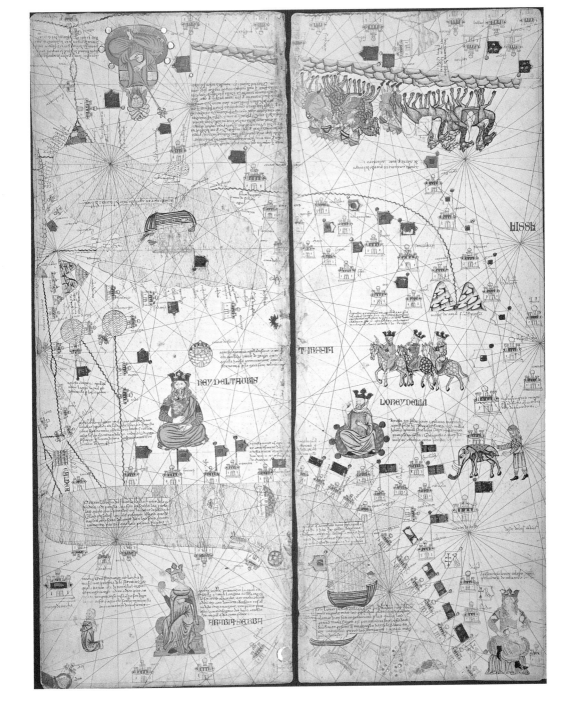

Maritime trade and commerce: Julfar and Jumeirah

The seafaring tradition of the UAE is ancient and rich, inextricably entwined with the area's cultural development. That ships left the ancient ports of the UAE for many far-flung destinations is attested to both by historical documents and by the results of archaeological excavations. Prior to the coming of Islam, successive empires had long plied and to some extent controlled the sea-routes to southern Arabia, Africa, India, south-west Asia and China. These flourishing diplomatic and commercial contacts, inherited by the Arabs, were stimulated by Muslim conquests of so much of the Middle and Near East and central and southern Asia. Domination of the seas by Arab navies made the Mediterranean, the Gulf, the Red Sea and the northern Indian Ocean into 'Arab lakes' for centuries.

Thus the Arabs achieved a virtual monopoly over the trade from East to West, becoming the middle-men who transported the export produce of the former, spices (especially pepper), precious stones, silk, fine ceramics and other luxury goods, to the Levant and beyond from their entrepôts on the Batinah, Arabian Gulf and Red Sea coasts. Ideas and technology such as the compass and the paper and porcelain manufacturing processes also found their way from China to Europe via the Arabs. There were two main routes from China to the West, one to the Gulf which took at least 18 months, and the other to the Red Sea ports. Arab goods exported to China included frankincense; in 1077 the amount exported to Canton reportedly amounted to over 170,000 kilograms.

The seafarers of what is now the United Arab Emirates played a major part in that process. The most compelling body of evidence for this trade comes from the results of the archaeological excavations of the town and district of Julfar in the modern Emirate of Ras al-Khaimah.

The port of Julfar is first mentioned by the Arab historian Al-Tabari in the context of early Islam in 637, as the port from which a Muslim fleet set sail to the coast of Fars, thus launching the conquest and overthrow of Sasanid Persia. This suggests that Julfar was already a major port, with the capacity to harbour and supply a considerable army (around 3000 men) and fleet. While Al-Tabari refers to Julfar as a port rather than a district it is clear that the name is also used in later times to refer to the whole district (probably the fertile alluvial plain at the foot of the Hajar mountains at the entrance to Wadi Bih in which the modern town of Ras al-Khaimah is situated). Yakut, the tenth century Arab historian, referred to Julfar as a fertile region rather than a town. Archeological evidence suggests that by the late seventeenth century, the urban site at al-Mataf had been largely abandoned, yet the local ruler is referred to as the 'Emir of Julfar. The maps made by the famous Danish explorer Carsten Niebuhr who journeyed around the Gulf from 1761-67 still show Julfar. However, by this time the bulk of the population had moved to the growing centre of Ras al-Khaimah, first mentioned in the late fifteenth century by the navigator Ahmed ibn Majid, himself a native of Julfar, which was situated on an easily defensible sandspit to the south of the site of medieval Julfar. The name Julfar probably continued in use for some time as a synonym for the area as a whole, and indeed the name remains firmly entrenched in the memory of the local inhabitants.

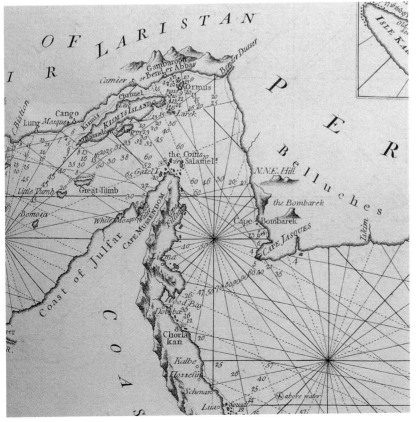

A chart of the Gulf from 1781 which is based on Carsten Niebuhr's remarkable map.

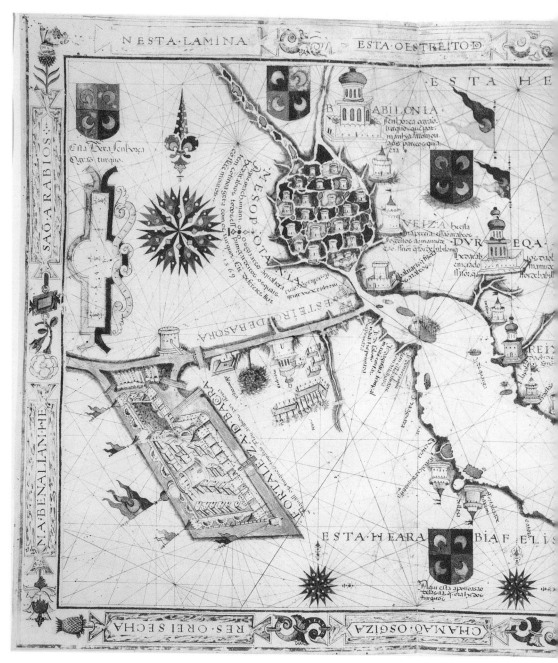

Fifteenth sheet of the Atlas 1568, presented to the Dukes of Alba, Bibioteca Duques de Alba, Palacio de Liria, Madrid. Note illustration of fortress at Julfar.

This shift in the focus of urban settlement was no new phenomenon. The actual location of the port of Julfar had moved at least once before in its history. As already noted, the first site seems likely to have been the tell of Kush, now some distance inland from the coast. There was also more possibly extra-mural settlement in the pre- and early-

The Waves of Time

Islamic period on the ancient sandbar at al-Hulaylah. The Kush site shows evidence of habitation certainly from the second to the early fourteenth century and the reason for its abandonment may lie in the geology of the region. The site seems to have been situated on the shore of an ancient lagoon which silted up at some point in the past. Kennet plans to test the possibility that there was at some point sufficient draught to provide mooring for large vessels by checking the depth and age of the lagoon deposits. The subsequent silting up of the lagoon could then be seen to have provided the impetus for relocating the port in the early fourteenth century to the site at al-Mataf, then, as now, on the beach to the north of the old town of Ras al-Khaimah.

The site at al-Mataf was identified by Hansman during his archaeological investigations in the early 1980s as the main urban site of late medieval Julfar, along with a subsidiary site at al-Nudud, which had also been investigated by an Iraqi team. Both sites produced evidence of occupation dating from the fourteenth to the seventeenth century, after which they seem to have faded. Following on from this, a major international expedition composed of British, French, German and Japanese archaeological teams was mounted in 1989. The work is still in progress and its final reports will provide a major contribution to our understanding of Julfar's history and role in the maritime trade of the period, with far-reaching consequences of international importance.

Whatever the reason for the shift in location, the combined sites of Kush and al-Mataf (early and late Julfar) provide an unbroken sequence from the first to the seventeenth century, during which the port of Julfar was evidently a major centre of international trade. This trade is most impressively documented by the pottery assemblage from these sites. Wares manufactured in East Africa, Yemen, Persia, Iraq, India, Thailand, Vietnam, and China have been identified. These include porcelain of the highest quality (and therefore cost), indicating the huge trade network and wealth of the port and citizens of Julfar. There are several historical references to the international importance and wealth of the town and its people. The Portuguese writer Duarte Barbosa remarked in 1517 of the population (Hansman 1985: p 10) that they were:

persons of great worth, great navigators (of course ibn Majid came from Julfar) and wholesale dealers - the trade of this place brings in a great revenue to the King of Hormuz.

This economic welfare, however, does not appear to have been constant. 'Boom and bust' episodes recognisable in the archaeological assemblage (including other evidence such as food resources and coins) reflect the historical realities of the time. The Gulf experienced hard times during the tenth century following the suppression of the last al-Julanda revolt of 892 and the subsequent devastation inflicted on the area by the Abbasid General Mohammed bin Nur. There were problems again from the eleventh century. Internal chaos caused by the gradual disintegration of the Abbasid empire effectively closed the trade route through the Gulf as Egypt became the population and power centre of the Islamic world, diverting trade through the Red Sea direct to Egyptian ports. The coastal town of Jumeirah in Dubai Emirate, for example, which flourished until the ninth or tenth century, seems to have faded after this time. More information on the site will become available when al-Qandeel publishes the results of excavations there, while the Kush excavations are also yielding promising results. The initial disruption created by the Mongol invasions of Central Asia and the Near East in the thirteenth century caused further hardship, culminating in 1258 with the murder of the Caliph and the sack of Baghdad, to which much of the trade through the Gulf had been previously directed.

The Waves of Time

The move from Kush to al-Mataf at Julfar seems to have coincided with the subsequent economic upturn at the beginning of the fourteenth century and this upturn is mirrored in the pottery assemblage from the sites, which shows a marked increase in the amount of imported Chinese fine wares, including porcelain and celadon. The diet of the inhabitants also reflects economic fortunes, with seafood dominating in the 'hard times', while cereals and meat appear in flourishing trade conditions.

Another find from the Kush site has caused a minor sensation. This is the discovery of coffee beans in an apparently twelfth century context. If confirmed, it would be the earliest evidence of the consumption of coffee yet discovered, pre-dating the first historical references to the crop's cultivation in Yemen. Coffee would have been a luxury product in the twelfth century, as the Yemeni producers certainly had a monopoly over its production and trade. The finding of Yemeni 'mustard ware' pottery (so-called because of the colour, not the contents!) with the coffee beans confirms such a trade connection at this time.

The almost total absence of coinage from the Kush site reflects the fact that no base metal coinage was circulated in the Gulf during the period so far investigated, the tenth to the thirteenth century. One perfectly preserved gold coin was however found, a tiny Omani quarter dinar of the tenth century.

From the beginning of the fourteenth century, the increasingly powerful Kings of Hormuz based on the eponymous island on the opposite side of the straits of that name began to control the flow of trade through the Gulf. Hormuz became one of the main ports on the Arabian Gulf for the trade to and from India and China. The Kings of Hormuz exercised direct control over Julfar for more than 300 years (see the remark by Duarte Barbosa quoted above), though they themselves had to pay tribute to the Portuguese from 1515. They are known to have operated a customs post at Julfar, profiting from the trade of the port which began to flourish again at this time. Most of the coinage found during the excavations at the al-Mataf site was struck at the Hormuz mint at Jarun (Old Hormuz). Their control was periodically challenged by the rulers from inland Persia, who sought the lucrative Gulf trade for themselves.

Archaeological evidence of the Hormuzi and Persian presences at Julfar from the early fourteenth century is provided by several sites, including the 'military camps' relating to the short-lived eighteenth century occupation of the area (1736-49) by the troops of Nadir Shah discussed by Hansman, and by the finding of a large fort at Julfar on the al-Mataf site, excavated by the French team.

This fort at al-Mataf is very likely that mentioned in an account of a battle in 1621 between local forces and the Portuguese and their Hormuzi vassals. The latter are reported to have bombarded the fort from their ships and to have set up a cannon in a nearby mosque. This mosque was probably that excavated by the British team, situated a short distance to the north of the fort. The mosque had been rebuilt no less than four times on the same spot from the fourteenth to the seventeenth century, emphasising the continuity of occupation here.

The fact that Julfar was the site of so many battles shows how crucial was control of the town for the powers in the region. The size and strength of the city wall of late Julfar at the al-Mataf site, excavated by the German team led by Janssen, is also an indicator of this. The wall was 1.5 metres thick, built of mud-brick and stone and has been calculated by Janssen to have originally stood at least 4 metres high.

Inscribed copper plate from Julfar.

The Portuguese era

The Portuguese were the first Europeans to exert their power over the coastline of the Gulf and Batinah coasts of Arabia, following Vasco da Gama's discovery of the Indian Ocean route during his voyage to Calicut on the west (Malabar) coast of India in 1498. The identity of his guide, the 'Gujerati Moor' later erroneously claimed to have been the great Emirati navigator Ahmed ibn Majid himself, is still unknown. Despite the fact that this first voyage was extremely costly in terms of men and materials (only two ships out of four and a third of the original crew made it back to Lisbon, with scurvy taking a heavy toll), da Gama was quickly able to convince the Portuguese king of the economic potential of his discovery of the route to India, even if there was disappointment over his failure to bring back very much valuable cargo. (There were also, of course, religious benefits in that the Portuguese, having helped to expel the Muslims from the Iberian Peninsula, now had a means of penetrating the heartland of Islam.) Two trading routes were used, the northern 'Silk Route' and the land and sea passage which crossed the Indian Ocean, passed through the Arabian Gulf, finally traversing the Levant; goods conveyed by the latter route had, up to now, ended up in the hands of the merchants of Venice and (to a lesser extent), those of Florence and Genoa. For the commercially hungry Portuguese, breaking the trade monopoly of their catholic co-religionists in Italy was of vital importance.

A *Portuguese cannon from the fort in Dubai.*

Discovery was followed by military conquest, as the Portuguese caraveloes with their high sides, gun-decks and heavier cannon proved more than a match for the Arab and Indian vessels with which they came into contact. Da Gama proceeded with the utmost determination and brutality. He had originally been chosen for the task of finding the route to India ahead of the more experienced seaman Bartolemeo Diaz because of his reputation as a hard man capable of maintaining discipline on such a long and hazardous voyage; Diaz had been forced to turn back from the euphemistically-titled 'Cape of Good Hope' by his mutinous crew after running into storms there. Da Gama employed his talents in this respect towards dominating the Indian Ocean, and the Portuguese activity at this early stage can be described as simple piracy. Trading with the Arabs and Indians for the luxury goods so sought after in the West was not a realistic proposition as the latter disobligingly

showed no interest in the goods the Portuguese had to offer. Da Gama therefore concluded that control of the already existing trade by military force was the only solution. He embarked on the task with enthusiasm. After terrorising the local traders and inhabitants by looting and burning their ships (with their inhabitants, regardless of sex or age), the Portuguese set about attacking key ports along the western Indian coast, beginning with Calicut in 1503. A ruthless response to any resistance encountered made subsequent conquests progressively easier, though the 'Moors' continued valiantly to resist, inflicting several defeats on their tormentors as the Portuguese relentlessly consolidated their control. Da Gama finally retired as Governor of Cochin in India, and died there a very wealthy man.

In 1506, a new viceroy and governor for Portugal's growing Indian Ocean possessions, Alfonso da Albuquerque, was appointed. His biography gives us graphic and fascinating (if rather one-sided) accounts of the Portuguese empire-building activities at this time. Da Albuquerque arrived in the Indian Ocean with instructions to blockade the Red Sea to Venetian and Egyptian trade, establishing a base on the island of Socotra. He then made for the centre of Gulf trade, Hormuz, sacking along the way those ports which did not yield to him. One was the UAE's east coast port of Khor Fakkan, then clearly an important commercial centre, described by Da Albuquerque as 'a very large place'. Its inhabitants included many merchants from Gujerat in India. He also recorded the existence of large estates in the mountains with a variety of citrus fruit plantations. Archaeological surveys of nearby mountain *wadis* like Wadi Safad, have identified the presence of large and sophisticated terraced field systems that may be a distant echo of Da Albuquerque's description. The town of Wadi Fakkan was torched before the Viceroy left and many of its inhabitants either captured or put to the sword. Only now, nearly 500 years later, has it once again become an important regional centre for maritime trade.

Moving on to India, Da Albuquerque meted out similarly tough treatment. Here is a description of his treatment of Goa after its inhabitants rebelled in 1510 against Portuguese control (Da Albuquerque 1774: Vol.III):

after the city had been pillaged, Alfonso da Albuquerque told the captains to reconnoitre the whole of the island and to put to the sword all the Moors, men, women and children, that should be found, and to give no quarter to any of them - for four days continuously they poured out the blood of the Moors who were found therein; and it was ascertained that of men, women, and children, the number exceeded six thousand.

By 1515, the Portuguese had overpowered all of the ports on the eastern Arabian coastline and had reduced the kindgom of Hormuz to vassaldom, extending their control as far as the head of the Gulf. They quickly imposed tolls on the flow of trade throughout the area. Ships were forced to pay for licences issued by the Portuguese, while traders had to unload their goods for resale from their 'factories' (*feitoria*).

The Portuguese built a string of forts along the Batinah and Gulf coast to consolidate their control of the Indian Ocean and Gulf trade, including ones at Julfar, Khor Fakkan, Bidiya and Dibba in UAE territory. The imposing fort at Dibba, a major port and trading post since pre-Islamic times, was typical of the Portuguese style of military architecture (still to be seen at Bahrain, Sohar and Muscat), with massive round corner towers designed to withstand artillery attack. An interesting description of the Dibba fort dates from 1646 (Kennet 1995: p 6):

The fortress at Doba (Dibba) is built in the shape of a square with four round bastions in the corners and an artillery tower (cavalro) in the middle with a well. Each wall is seven bracas long and four in height and eleven palmos in width. It is made of stone and has parapets. Inside the fortress there is a house for the Captain, a Church and an underground warehouse for ammunition; there are hollow spaces among the bastions for storing provisions. As well as this the fortress

has an outer fence which is very long and is built in the shape of a square with five bastions, one of them over the gate and the other four in the corners. The gate is used as a guard's quarters. Each wall is 25 bracas long and two and a half bracas high; it is made of adobe with loopholes because there are no parapets. There are houses for the soldiers inside this enclosure.

Overleaf:
Chart of Arabia and the Eastern Mediteranean, part of a Portolan Atlas c. 1650 at British Library, London.

Sadly, no trace of this imposing structure has yet been found.

Although the Gulf Arabs reportedly had artillery before the arrival of the Portuguese, the larger destructive power of the European's ship-mounted cannons caused the Arabs to rethink their own defences. Portuguese innovations such as the use of stone as a building material were assimilated into the local defensive architecture, while the forts

of the later rulers at Abu Dhabi, Dubai, Ajman, Umm al-Qaiwain and Ras al-Khaimah are positioned so as to dominate the harbours of these towns. Portuguese forts likewise dominated the port harbours, enforcing control of the shipping using them. This was indeed the main concern of the Portuguese, whose power and wealth depended on their ability to control such major trading centres and military strongpoints with a relatively small navy and army.

The Portuguese were finally expelled from the Batinah coast by local inhabitants and the Omanis and from Hormuz by a coalition of the Persians, and, a sign of things to come, the English. They managed to hold on to Julfar till 1633, building a new fort there (since disappeared) in 1631, most probably as a base from which to recapture Hormuz, an objective they failed to accomplish. The site of al-Mataf seems to have been abandoned around this time.

Despite the almost exclusively predatory nature of their power in the Gulf, the Portuguese left a tangible legacy behind them both in the field of architecture and in ship-building.

ARABIA
DESERTA

TROPICO

EQVINOC

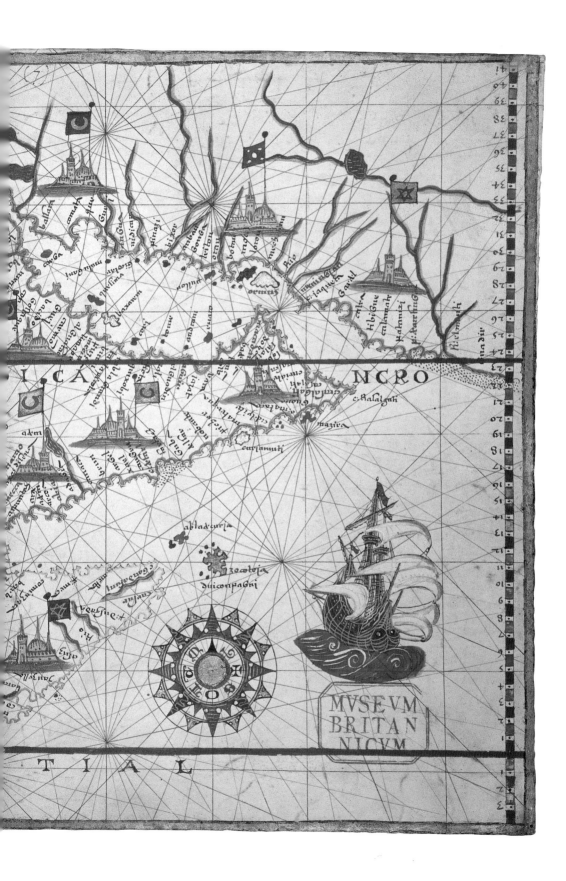

MVSEVM
BRITAN
NICVM

The late Islamic period;
the rise of the al–Qasimi and the Bani Yas

With the expulsion of the Portuguese from the Gulf and the subsequent departure of the Persian and Omani forces after 1633, the local dynasty of the al-Qasimi, based at Sharjah and the new port of Ras al-Khaimah to which the inhabitants of Julfar now moved, began to develop their own seaborne power in the Gulf. They gradually established control not only of large sections of the Arabian Gulf and Batinah coasts from Sharjah to Kalba, but also of the opposite shore,

Map of Arabia from Katib Chelebi's 'jihan-numa', 1728.

The Waves of Time

establishing major trading entrepòts at Qishm island and Lingah on the Persian coast. (Lingah later became the main stopping off point for British ships passing through the Gulf, crucially losing this role to Dubai in the late nineteenth century, presaging the latter's rise to its present importance).

The activities of the Qawasim come sharply into focus as their interests clash with those of the British. The British had consolidated their power in India by the beginning of the nineteenth century and looked upon any activity which could be regarded as a disturbance to their trade and supply routes to the subcontinent with active displeasure. Roused by the Qawasim's attacks on ships under British protection, they branded the Qawasim's activities as piracy and resolved to solve the problem of the 'Pirate coast.' Accordingly they launched an expedition in 1809 against the main al-Qasimi base at Ras al-Khaimah, which ensured a short period of peace. However, the Qawasim rashly asserted themselves again in the years that followed, enforcing their right to levy tolls on shipping using the Gulf and raiding those who refused to accept this, including ships under British protection. Finally, in 1819 the British sent a strong naval and land force from Bombay to Ras al-Khaimah, destroying the Qawasim fleet, burning the town itself and reducing the fortifications in the area by siege, notably the forts at Ras al-Khaimah and Dhayah near Sharm. Again it was the superior artillery of the Europeans that secured the victory over the Arab forces, with 24-pounder cannons from the ships being dragged ashore and employed against the mud-brick fortifications to devastating effect, as this report from a British officer present at the attack demonstrates (Kennet 1995):

It being found that our 12 and 18-pounders produced but a slight impression on the walls and towers, while the enemy availed themselves of our own shot to annoy us greatly, as they fitted exactly the calibre of their own guns, it was resolved that several 24-pounders should be erected as a breaching battery. Two 24-pounders were accordingly landed, with considerable exertion, from the 'Liverpool' and had to be dragged a long way through deep sand. The 24-pounders opened on the 8th (of December) with marked effect, and the walls and towers appeared to shake and totter under the force of the shot.

The Emirates of Abu Dhabi and Dubai can be traced in their origins from at least the sixteenth century onwards, with the emergence of the Bani Yas tribal confederation as the dominant power in the region. From around the sixteenth century, extensive evidence of occupation of the islands of Abu Dhabi has been identified by archaeological surveys, while the names of a number of islands, including Sir Bani Yas, Zirku, Qarnein, Das and Dalma appear in a list published by the court jeweller of the Srene Republic of Venice, Gasparo Balbi, in 1580.

Map of Maritime Arabia, 1855.

While an apparent lacuna in information on settlement of the islands during the early and mid-Islamic periods has yet to be explained, the numerous late Islamic sites indicate that many islands were settled seasonally, and, in some cases, permanently from the sixteenth century onwards. Important evidence has been found of both pearling and fishing, for example, on the islands of Balghelam, Merawah and Sir Bani Yas. Such settlement may well have been originally connected with a growth in the importance of the pearl trade, which had originally prompted Balbi to visit the area in search of new sources to satisfy what may have been an expanding market in post-renaissance Europe.

While some inhabitants of the coast and islands, such as the Rumaithat sub-section of the Bani Yas confederation, may have traditionally been engaged in both pearling and fishing, a clear pattern can now be traced of sections of nomadic desert and oasis dwellers also visiting the coast at certain times of the year to join in the pearling.

In the case of Dalma which, unusually, was well supplied with fresh water springs, permanent settlement occurred from at least the Ubaid (Neolithic) period onwards. The past importance of Dalma is further underlined by the survival on the island of an impressive group of nineteenth century buildings, which include three mosques and a large pearl merchant's house. Dalma appears to have been a major centre

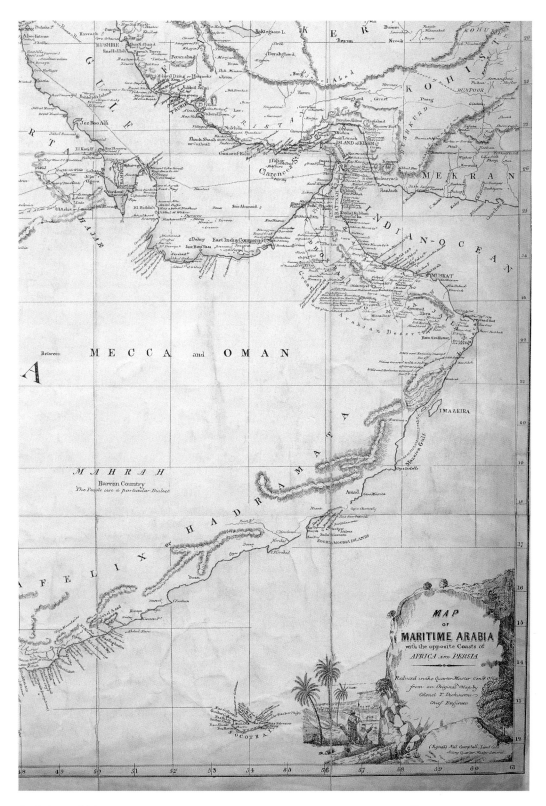

MAP
OF
MARITIME ARABIA
with the opposite Coasts of
AFRICA and PERSIA

Reduced in the Quarter-Master Gen.l Office
from an Original Map by
Colonel T. Dickinson
Chief Engineer

of the pearling industry, with records of merchants coming from as far away as Bombay to negotiate with the pearl-divers, while extensive scatters of oriental porcelain potsherds from at least the fourteenth century onwards are further testimony to the involvement of the island in the maritime trade of the Gulf region.

Nearby Sir Bani Yas, site of an important Christian monastic settlement in the late pre-Islamic period, appears to have been used subsequently only on an occasional basis by fishermen and by herdsmen from the mainland, who would bring their livestock across in the winter months. Even these semi-nomadic visitors were not isolated from the patterns of regional trade. Several Late Islamic camp sites have been identified on the island, one of which, at Ras Danan in the north, contains not only circles of stones, probably tent weights, and remains of fireplaces littered with dugong and turtle bones, but also sherds of imported oriental porcelain, suggesting a curiously evocative picture of simple herdsmen and fishermen drinking from fine Chinese teacups. There are also signs of recent more permanent settlement, including house foundations and a graveyard with graves most unusually marked out by dugong bones.

Merawah has also been inhabited intermittently since the Stone Age, the presence of sweet water again being an attraction. There are graveyards, old house foundations and a mosque, all dating to the last centuries before oil. Of particular interest is the use of driftwood as a building material, an example of the resourcefulness of the local inhabitants in this harsh part of the world.

The island of Balghelam is covered with signs hinting at permanent or semi-permanent settlement in the recent past, with numerous large hearths, wells, and middens with material dating from the eighteenth century. Shell middens, with oyster shells reflecting the importance of the pearling industry, are common features of the westernmost islands, including Ghagha, Humr, Ufsa'iyyah and the Yasats.

A recurring feature on many of the islands are simple rows of stones defining a large internal area, interpreted, because of their Mihrab (prayer niche) facing towards the holy city of Mecca, as Eid Mosques. These could accommodate several hundred people, more than the islands themselves could ever have supported. It is possible that the crews of the fishing and pearling fleets gathered here to pray communally on the important occasions of the Islamic year.

The population seems to have declined on all the islands with the collapse of the pearl market in the 1920s, suggesting that the local tribes began to drift back to the mainland, returning only in the winter to fish as they had in the past.

The marine heritage of the United Arab Emirates in the Islamic period can be seen to be rich and varied, being a component part of the heritage of the Arabs and the Orient, while maintaining certain unique characteristics. The fact that so much of the country borders on the sea means that it has always been a cross-roads of cultures and an important staging post for goods and ideas, while still maintaining its own special character and traditions; as it continues to do today.

Ahmed ibn Majid

Arabian navigator, explorer and poet

Peter Vine and
Peter Hellyer

They have the 'compass' and they have lines describing miles and their rhumbs are eight heads of al-Zauj and between these are eight more. All the sixteen have names of stars in the Egyptian and Maghribi languages... .

We use 32 rhumbs and we have tirfa, zam and qiyas (measurements of star altitude) but they are not able to do these things nor can they understand the things which we do although we can understand what they do and we can use their knowledge and travel in their ships. ...We can easily travel in their ships and upon their sea so some have magnified us in this business and look up to us for it. They acknowledge that we have the better knowledge of the sea and its sciences and the wisdom of the stars in the high roads of the sea, and the knowledge of the division of the ship in length and breadth. For we divide the ship in length and breadth according to the compass rose and we have measurements of star altitudes. They have no similar division or any means of dividing from the prow of the ship to guide themselves; neither do they use star altitude measurements to guide them when they incline to the right or left. Hence they have to acknowledge that we know best in that.

The Waves of Time

So wrote the renowned sailor, navigator, explorer and poet, Ahmed ibn Majid, in 1488 before Vasco da Gama ever rounded the Cape of Good Hope, or set foot on the Arabian lands from which Ibn Majid, his equally skilled father, grandfather and other forebears had been sailing and exploring throughout their working lives. The 'they' of whom he wrote were, of course, Europeans and it is true to say that the Arabs had sailed into European waters long before the Europeans had mastered the art of crossing the

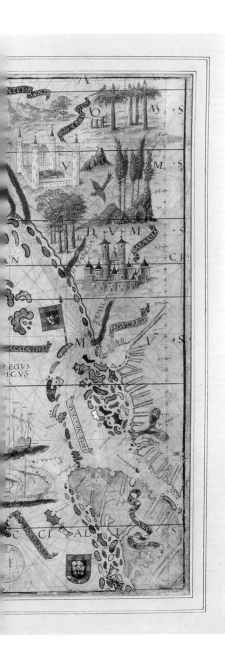

Indian Ocean. Arab vessels used to sail throughout the Mediterranean and much further afield and the Indian Ocean trade was dependent upon their maritime skills of boat-building, seamanship and navigation, already thousands of years old when Ibn Majid put pen to paper.

Evidence of the skills of the boatbuilders and navigators of the Gulf region stretches far back into prehistory. Early texts from the Sumerian civilisation in the third millennium BC have been interpreted as evidence of ships being built in Magan (Oman and the UAE) for the Indian Ocean trade, so well attested to on archaeological sites throughout the Emirates. Over 6000 years ago, the people of the Emirates were connected with a marine commercial network that reached up to Mesopotamia, while over 4000 years ago, there was a link with the civilisations of the Indus Valley, both precursors of a tradition of involvement in maritime commerce that continues today.

Arabia and India, from the Miller Atlas *by Pedro Reinel, c. 1519. Bibliotheque Nationale, Paris.*

While the early sailors and navigators doubtless came from countries all the way around the coastlines of the Indian Ocean, the people of the Emirates must always have been an integral part of that community. In his chapter on the pre-Islamic maritime heritage of the UAE, Potts shows that the inhabitants of the Emirates knew about lateen sails long before the technique reached Europe. Ibn Majid, though unquestionably one of the most celebrated of the Arab navigators of the Middle Ages, was, for all his skills, the successor to a heritage that stretched back thousands of years before he was born. He remains, as he should, a source of pride for the seafarers of the country today.

Ibn Majid's reputation as a navigator, long neglected by scholars but now attracting an increasing amount of attention, is based firmly upon 40 surviving works, 39 of them in the form of poems, some short, but others, such as the 805 verse *al-Sofaliya* describing the sea route from India to Sofala on the coast of Mozambique, of great length. One treatise only was in prose, *Kitab al-Fawa'id fi usul ilm al-bahr wa'l-qawa'ia*, (the *Fawa'id* for short), *or The Book of Profitable Things Concerning the First Principles and Rules of Navigation*. Completed in 1490, it is a lengthy opus which not only summarises all of Ibn Majid's own knowledge of navigation, but also draws extensively on the work of early Arab astronomers with relation to those stars used in navigation.

Tibbetts, whose study of Ibn Majid and translation of the *Fawa'id* remains the best source, rightly describes the book as 'the key work to the study of Ibn Majid's art, if not to the whole science of Indian Ocean navigation.'.

Ibn Majid himself was born in the town of Julfar, close to present-day Ras al-Khaimah in the United Arab Emirates, around the period 1432–37. He came from a long line of sailors and navigators. Indeed much of the raison d'être for his writing was to update and correct navigational notes of his father Majid bin Mohammed, and of his grandfather Muhammad ibn 'Umar who was actively sailing the Indian Ocean in the early part of the fifteenth century. Ahmed ibn Majid, commonly known as just Ibn Majid, possessed, as remains customary among the people of Arabia, a detailed oral history of his ancestry. He refers to this in the beginning of the *Fawa'id* when he describes his lineage as follows: Shihab al-Din Ahmad bin Majid bin Muhammad bin 'Umar bin Fadl bin Duwaik, bin Yusuf bin Hasan bin Husain bin Abi Ma'laq al-Sa'di bin Abi Raka'ib al Najdi. This list must have stretched back to the late thirteenth century, around 1280 AD. He also describes himself as belonging to the Qais 'Ailan, indicating that his family originally came from Nejd in central Arabia. In common with many other tribes, they must have migrated from this area to the eastern coastline of the peninsula, moving down into the Emirates, where Ibn Majid's family settled in Julfar, already an important port at the very beginning of the Islamic era. From there, presumably, his grandfather and later his father

The Waves of Time

took up the profession of pilot, ranging far and wide beyond the Arabian Gulf itself.

Ibn Majid's father was an expert in navigating boats up the Red Sea, a route that is notoriously difficult, requiring a considerable amount of tacking against the wind. His detailed knowledge of the shores of both Arabia and Sudan were acknowledged by other sailors who gave him the nickname: Mu'allim al-Barrain, which translates as 'the pilot of two coasts'. An island in the Red Sea was named after him.

By the time Vasco da Gama did sail around the Cape of Good Hope and bring the Portuguese vessels into the Indian Ocean, Ibn Majid had hung up his sailing clothes and was approaching the end of his days. His last known poem was written in 906 AH (1500 AD) and it is believed that he died soon after that, at a little over 70 years old.

These facts did not however prevent him from becoming the victim of a baseless, but influential attack by the Meccan author Qutb al-Din al-Nahrawali. This writer, born in 1511, several years after the death of Ibn Majid, and who wrote his account of the Ottoman conquest of Yemen in the mid-sixteenth century, accused Ibn Majid of being the sailor who

Map of East Africa, Arabia, Western India and Madagascar, from a Portolan Atlas by Diego Homen, c. 1558 (vellum). British Library, London.

Sightings of seabirds were an important factor in navigation

had treacherously divulged to the Portuguese the hard-earned knowledge of the Arabian sailors; knowledge without which Portuguese vessels could not have navigated the route between East Africa and India, across the Indian Ocean. The fact that Ibn Majid was close to death at this time was not considered, nor was the fact that the Portuguese themselves refer to the sailor who first guided their boats around the Seychelles bank and showed them how to reach India as an Arab from India, known to them by the name of 'Malemo Cana' or 'Malemo Canaqua'. These names probably derived from the word used for pilot throughout the northern

Indian Ocean at that time: *mu'allim* or *malim* and the Indian for astrologer, *kanaka*. In their own accounts the Portuguese clearly state that their navigator was from Gujerat in India whereas Ibn Majid was notably proud of his own Arab ancestry.

Few now give the slightest credence to the notion that Ibn Majid helped the Portuguese in any way, although the skills of which he was an unexcelled master were undeniably revealed to da Gama and his successors by some other unknown pilot.

Ibn Majid himself certainly did not believe in making life too easy for those who would try to steal local knowledge for their own gain. In writing about the Red Sea he states that there were many important facts that he would not write down for public use

> *lest ignorant men fall upon them and discuss them with learned men and thus wrongly acquire the knowledge of the measurements of this sea and its islands. We have left them out here so that someone will have to travel a great deal in order to know about it.*

Does this sound like a man who would give freely of his knowledge to foreigners who invaded the waters through which he and his family had been sailing for generations?

> *For I would have known nothing about it had not my grandfather – the mercy and pardon of God upon him – been well versed in this sea and my father – God have mercy on him and pardon him – added still more to his knowledge.*

In his translation and discussion of Ibn Majid's texts, Tibbetts dismisses the idea that Ibn Majid would have parted so lightly with such a wealth of knowledge to Vasco da Gama when disclosure was bound to cause debilitating competition for Arabian traders, quite apart from the terrible suffering and deprivation which actually ensued. Tibbetts points out that Sidi Celebi, an Ottoman Admiral of the mid-sixteenth century who sought, unsuccessfully, to expel the Portuguese from Arabia and India, and who was a contemporary of Qutb al-Din al-Nahrawali, referred to Ibn Majid as a nautical writer but never once mentioned him in connection with the arrival of the Portuguese.

In summarising his view on the falsehood of al-Nahrawali's assumptions, Tibbetts states:

> It is much more likely that the pilot of Vasco da Gama was an Indian stranded in Africa, hoping to earn his passage back to his native land than an Arab of

Ibn Majid's knowledge who would have realised the consequences of introducing the cursed Franks into the Indian Ocean trade. If the political consequences of this deed were ever thought out beforehand and I am sure that Ibn Majid would have thought of them, it can only have been some man from one of the continually warring Indian states hoping to boost his own country's fortunes at the expense of a neighbour. The Arab who had everything to lose by introducing more competition would never have done such a thing.

Ibn Majid's great achievements should not have been clouded by the false accusations that were laid against him after his death and it is fitting that we now have an opportunity to celebrate his works and to recognise the great gift of Arabian maritime lore of which he was a part. The art of Arabian navigation benefited not only the people of Arabia and surrounding lands, but also the European sailors who entered their waters with a determination to take control of the sea-routes between India and Europe.

What sort of man was Ibn Majid? How much of his knowledge came from personal experience and how much from word of mouth? Is it

Ibn Majid was acutely aware that careless navigation could spell disaster for vessel and crew.

possible to overcome the concealments and distortions of time and reconstruct the character of such a unique person? The answer to all of these questions lies in his own writing, for Ibn Majid wrote not only about the art of navigation but also about his own experiences and his own views on life. We are fortunate indeed that his manuscripts have survived for they offer a window through which we can indeed see the man himself.

First and foremost he was a practical man, a man whose education was based as much on personal experience as upon any formal training. His classroom was the sea itself and his teachers were his own close relatives and colleagues with whom he shared the experiences of sailing on dhows that plied their trade through the Indian Ocean and up the Red Sea. Whilst his family home was in Julfar he seems to have spent much of his working life in Oman, for the navigation directions in his work are centred on Ras al-Hadd, on the coast of Oman, from where vessels set off for Africa, India or up the Red Sea. He spent long periods away from his family and mentions in his writing that this is one of the burdens a sailor has to face.

His writing also reveals a man who recognised the value of record keeping and who was fiercely proud of his own reputation. By nature a teacher, he felt that he had a duty to record his knowledge of navigation so that others could benefit from it. This was far more than a matter of generosity or a craving for respect among his colleagues. It was in fact a matter of life and death, both for him, his family, and for the sailors who used his notes to sail in waters that surveyors of the present century have described as 'unknown' or 'treacherous'. Unmarked reefs, shallow banks, and low-lying islands are predominant features of coastal Arabia and the Red Sea where Ibn Majid and his colleagues depended upon their navigational skills to bring sailing vessels safely to their destinations. A careless mistake could easily spell disaster for both vessel and its crew. Ibn Majid was acutely aware of this fact and often writes of the need to exercise caution:

> So practice this science and do not be neglectful or you will make an error which is destroying to both possessions and wealth . . . The errors of other studies are verbal only and they give you time for correcting mistakes, but this science gives you no time . . .

Ibn Majid was not shy about singing his own praises. He probably had every justification in regarding himself as the pre-eminent Arab navigator of his time and he made sure that his readers would recognise this:

> For I was Shihab as a bright star rising, whenever
> > The navigators gather to discuss my directions
> I have mentioned my name in this verse because of my unique knowledge of this sea.

Remarking on the difficulties inherent in carrying passengers or crew on board who do not understand the lore of the sea, Ibn Majid wrote the following verse:

> If I remain with those who do not follow in my steps
> It is more bitter than the dangers of a stormy sea.
> Give me a ship and I will take it through danger,
> For this is better than having friends who can be insincere.
> At times I will accompany it through difficulties,
> At other times I will divert myself with society and late nights.
> If there is no escape from society or from travelling
> Or riding the ship then we have surely reached our final end.

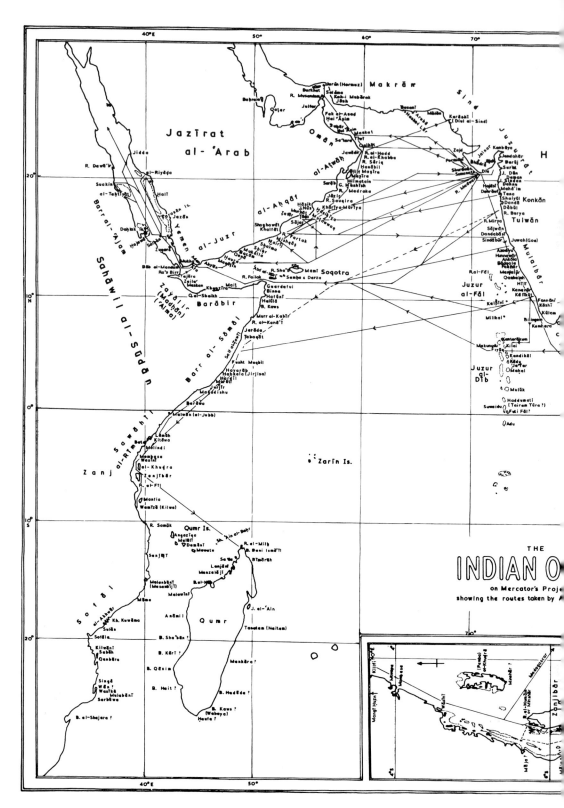

THE

INDIAN O

on Mercator's Proj

showing the routes taken by

The Waves of Time

Map of the
Indian Ocean
showing routes
taken by Ibn
Majid and other
Arab navigators.
Reproduced from
Arab
Navigation in
the Indian
Ocean before
the coming of
the Portuguese
by G.R. Tibbetts,
Royal Asiatic
Society, London,
1981.

The ship is a wonder of God, my mount, my escort.
Of Lord be generous in travel. 'tis the house of God itself.
I have exhausted my life for science and have been famous for it.
My honour has been increased by knowledge in my old age.
Had I not been worthy of this, kings would not have
Paid attention to me. This is the greatest aim achieved.

Navigation to Ibn Majid involved much more than a detailed knowledge of the stars and an ability to calculate latitude. Every sign of nature was also part of the equation, whether it be the shape of a mountain peak or the sight of a sea-bird:

The Umm al-Sanani is a blue bird with a white stomach dusted with blue. It is usually seen south of Socotra, but when you sail between Socotra and the mainland, you do not see it . . .

His eye was always on the sea and what it contained:

It is also possible to find around this bank much amber, for amber is not seen or found on any coast except around this place...Some say it is a sort of wax and some say it is the dung of a wild animal found in the islands around these places, they drop it onto the beach and it gets into the water, stays there a long time and fishes swallow it. God alone can give us information on this.

We now know of course that the valuable and much sought after amber comes from sperm whales that are still found in the region Ibn Majid mentions.

One of the most nerve-racking moments for any navigator is that first sight of land following a long sea-crossing, when excitement must give way to the discipline required to bring one's boat safely into an anchorage. Ibn Majid was well used to doing this and had learned that sailors spent far too much time discussing what might or might not be instead of quietly getting on with the task at hand:

So be certain of your ground with landfalls, for more errors appear when the talking is much, especially in this subject of ours (navigation). Then the errors from talking are more than the errors from doing.

Ibn Majid sailed to many far-off places in his time but always returned to Arabia, his beloved homeland. In the tenth fa'ida of his book he discusses the islands he had visited: Madagascar, Sumatra, Java, Al-

Ghur, Ceylon, Zanzibar, Bahrain, Hormuz and Qishm and, of course, Socotra which he interestingly describes as being inhabited by some 'ruffianly Christians' thought by some to be remnants of the Greeks.

In his ninth fa'ida, he briefly offers directions for a round-the-world tour, stretching from China to the Iberian peninsula, which he describes thus:

> Andalus, which is the nearest (i.e. furthest) to the west, belonging to both Islam and the Christian Franks, and in the time of writing this book, half of it belongs to Islam and half to the Christians.

Sadly, his *Kitab* offers little information about the Arabian Gulf, which he must have known well, perhaps because the navigators for whom he compiled his great work would have been too familiar with the Gulf to have required the information. Such description as is included, however, is immediately recognisable:

> When you have passed the Extensive Basra (going down the western side of the Gulf), the coast stretches to Salamiya (present-day Kuwait?), and to al-Qatif and al-Hasa and 'Oman Qatar all in the south east and along it are islands both inhabited and uninhabited and there are ports and the island of Bahrain is there which possesses a pearl fishery where approximately a thousand ships have been used for diving for centuries and this place is not surpassed. Around Bahrain there are a number of other islands, inhabited or not, with pearl fisheries, and from these to the limits of Musandam is a month by land and seven days by sea, (the coast), inclining a little to the north east,

– an accurate, if short, description of the Arabian Gulf coastline of the United Arab Emirates.

He never tired of learning, studying and listening to others. He was a man who only sought the truth about a situation. 'Wisdom is the ambition of the believer. So search out your ambition even from among the Unbelievers.' But he was also a romantic who enjoyed the beauty that he saw in all aspects of life. Frequently his writings evoke images of nature and the emotions of love:

> The turtledove sings on its branch, its voice
> sways with rapture, living yet tender

and later in the same poem:

> While the candle which was between us appeared,

As a silver spear with a jewelled tip.
While the tops of the trees waved above us,
Shaking as the hearts of cowards,
Until dawn gave us the morning,
And the worshipper had to hearken to the Mu'ezzin's voice.
Then the arrow struck us, separating us,
Is there a thing which time has not pierced?

Such poetry and imagery speaks to us clearly of a sensitive man and one for whom the quality of life was measured by values other than wealth or status. He loved to experience things at first hand and he also wanted to share his feelings and experiences with others. The fact that this brought him to local and regional eminence was not something to be denied but savoured, especially in his later years when he was less active on the physical level but had a host of experiences to recount and knowledge to share.

When Ibn Majid completed the *Fawa'id* in 895 AH (1490 AD) he wrapped it up in characteristic style, always aware that his mission was to impart knowledge rather than to theorise on matters beyond his understanding. He wrote:

I have summarised this section about the sea and the other ten sections so that a man can progress without finding the book and its teaching too long and so that it is not too heavy for the reader and the writer. As we have said in one of our poems:

When you find a thing right, do not harp on it
Without from it the reins of Commentary and the Pen

I have finished this book in the year 895 refraining from excessive speech. I have instructed you by the power of God to little speech and little sleep, and little food. We ask pardon of God for any exaggeration. Written with the help of God to whom be praise and with the goodness of his guidance, it is called 'Kitab al-Fawa'id - concerning the first principles and rules of navigation. Praise be to the one God.

Less than ten years after this Ibn Majid died, leaving behind him a legacy that was to inspire thousands of Arab sailors. His name was still being cited as an authority by sailors from as far away as the Maldives in the early nineteenth century, over 300 years after his death. To the very end he remained at heart a true seaman, to whom one would have had no hesitation in entrusting one's life – on sea or land. While his full contribution to Arab navigation, and, consequently, to the science of navigation has been little studied, the name of Ibn Majid, born over five centuries ago, remains well-known in his native Ras al-Khaimah, and his memory is inextricably linked with the pride of the people of the Emirates in their national marine heritage.

Of
Pearls
& Boats

Peter Vine and
Joseph Elders

THE PEARLING INDUSTRY on the Gulf coast of the UAE has a long recorded
history. It will probably never be known when the people of the Emirates
first began to harvest the pearls of the Gulf, but individual pearls have
been found in excavations on archaeological sites that date back to
at least the late stone age, six or seven thousand years ago.
Archaeologists believe that the 'fish eyes' from the Gulf, referred to
in ancient Babylonian cuneiform texts may well have been pearls. Al-
Idrisi mentions that in 1154 Julfar was already a major pearling centre.
The Portuguese writer Duarte Barbosa recorded in 1517 that: 'Here
(Julfar) is a very great fishery as well, of seed pearls as of large pearls;
and the Moors of Hormuz come hither to buy them and carry them
to India and many other lands.' The Portuguese traveller Pedro Teixeira
mentions that a fleet of 50 *terradas* sailed from Julfar every year to the
pearl beds. There was even a kind of pearl found near Julfar named
after the latter, and it was the growing interest of the Europeans in
Gulf pearls that led to the tour of the Venetian state jeweller, Gasparo
Balbi, in 1580. To the people of the Emirates, pearling offered a major,
if seasonal, form of employment and formed an important part of the
national economy. Indeed, the name, 'The Trucial States', by which
the UAE was formerly known, was derived from an annual series of

maritime truces agreed in the middle of the nineteenth century by the various rulers, at British prompting, that were designed to maintain peace at sea during the pearling season. While many of those engaged in the pearling industry would return home between seasons, there were others for whom it was a full time occupation. British historical records from the late nineteenth century, for example, refer to divers from the Emirates travelling to Sri Lanka to work on the pearl beds there once the season in the Gulf was over.

By the beginning of the twentieth century there were, according to Lorimer's calculation, over 1200 pearling boats operating out of the Trucial States, each carrying an average crew of 18 men. This meant that during the summer most able-bodied men, numbering more than 22,000, were absent on the pearl banks. The average annual value of pearls exported from the Gulf at the turn of the century was estimated at £1,434,399 with an additional £30,439 resulting from the export of mother-of-pearl. The industry reached its peak shortly before the undermining of the market by the Japanese development of cultured pearls in the 1920s. The perfection of this technique in response to the expanding market and huge demand for pearls (no fashionable young American or European woman of the period was to be seen without a long string of pearls around her neck) allowed the Japanese to flood the market with cheap pearls, making the 'real' pearls from the Gulf prohibitively expensive by comparison. The economic depression of the 1930s completed the destruction of the pearling industry, leading to a great deal of hardship, particularly in the coastal area of what is now Abu Dhabi, Qatar and Bahrain, where the local economy, from supplies for the pearling fleets to ship-building, was built around pearling. No substitute was found before the discovery of oil.

Pearling was never merely a trade or a means of subsistence for the population along the southern Gulf littoral. It was an entirely integrated social system which has left a rich heritage of traditions to be enjoyed by the indigenous population who are now benefiting from the security engendered by the discovery of oil after centuries of hardship. The pearl banks near the southern shores of the Gulf were not the particular domain of any individual sheikhdom, but were open to all pearling boats from Arab ports. The notion that these pearl banks belonged to the Arabs of the southern Gulf was, and is, deeply ingrained. Attempts by foreigners to exploit the resources have been thwarted in the last century and right up to the present time and indeed at one point, in an effort to protect the divers' livelihood, the British introduced a number of regulatory measures to the pearling profession. Outsiders were forbidden to engage in any pearling without the permission of the rulers and pearls were to be gathered only by the traditional practice of diving, for which the use of modern diving equipment was banned. Thus the time-honoured methods, first developed thousands of years ago, continued to survive until the demise of the industry itself.

The general term for the pearl fishery was *ghaus* (literally diving) and all the people that took part in the active operations were included under the common denomination (*ghawawis*). There were traditionally two pearl-diving seasons, the *ghaus al-bard*, the cold spring season, and the *ghaus al-kabir* in the summer (though other, shorter seasons might also be undertaken in the winter months).The method used in harvesting the pearl oyster (three separate species of oyster, occupying different habitats, secrete the nacreous material required to form the precious pearl) was much the same throughout the region and probably hadn't altered radically in thousands of years. A local pearling captain, appointed by the ruler in each port, set the date for sailing to and from the pearling banks. All the boats from the same port under the authority of one sheikh departed for the *ghaus al-kabir* at the beginning of June in one great picturesque swoop of sail, and returned to port together, approximately 120 days later, towards the end of September. *Sambuks* were mostly employed as pearling boats, but the *batil, barqarah, shu'ai* and *zarqah* also had a place in the industry. Depending on the preference

or particular strategy of the captain, a pearling boat might anchor for the entire season at one pearl bank or move from bank to bank. Short trips were made to ports such as the island of Dalma for the renewal of drinking-water, rice, dates, coffee and tobacco.

The normal complement of crew for the average pearling vessel was 18–20 men; eight divers or *ghasah* (sing. *ghais*), ten haulers *siyub* (sing. *saib*) and an apprentice *walaid* (pl. *aulad*) who fished, cooked, cleaned and took care of the coffee. A *nahham* was only employed on the larger boats, to co-ordinate the evocative rhythmical chants used to ease the rigorous tasks on board. The captain (*nukhada*), chose the location of the dive and also took control of the sale of the catch.

The Waves of Time

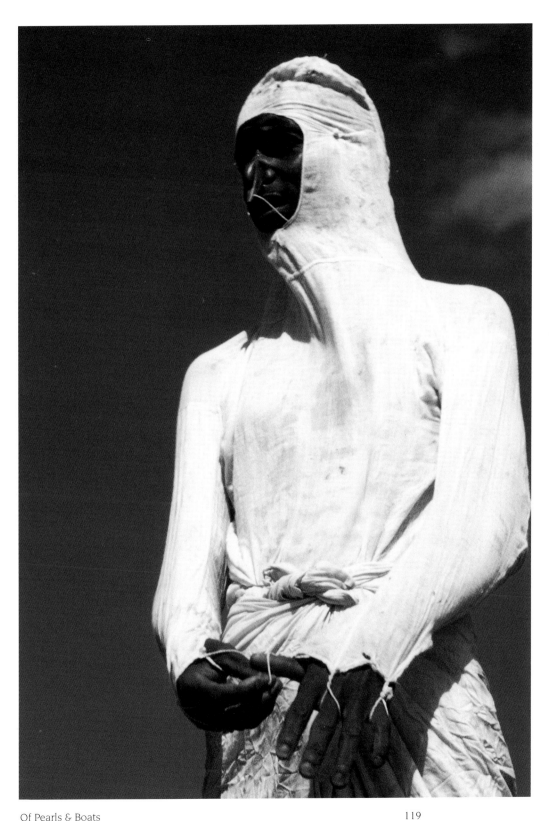

Despite much nostalgic reflection on the communal spirit encountered in pearling, there is no doubt that life was extremely hard for the average diver. Diving commenced about an hour after sunrise, the divers having breakfasted lightly on coffee and dates, and proceeded right through until an hour before sunset, except for prayers and sometimes coffee and a short rest at midday. The hard-working diver, nose pegged with clips of turtle shell (*ftam*) and ears plugged with wax, plummeted to the bottom with the aid of a stone (*hajar*) attached to his foot which was subsequently pulled up by his attendant hauler on board ship. Fingers protected by leather caps (*khabt*), he quickly filled an attached basket (*diyyin*) with as many shells as possible, finally signalling by a tug on his rope that he needed to be hauled to the surface. The diver rested in the water after his arduous task, holding onto his rope in characteristic pose, while his basket was being emptied, but it wasn't long before he was again descending to the deep. After an evening meal of fish and rice, complemented by dates and coffee, the crew attempted to settle down for the night on board the crowded deck to avail of any cooling sea breezes.

The Waves of Time

Not before the following dawn was the pile of oyster shells opened to reveal the previous day's catch. This task took place under the watchful eye of the captain who recorded any particularly big pearls that might be sold individually.

Some *nukhada* sold the season's catch to a *tawwash* who visited the pearl banks from time to time while the diving was in progress, some made direct contact with wholesale pearl merchants (*tujar*), whilst others contracted with financiers at a prearranged price. The wholesaler arranged for the sale of the pearls and mother-of-pearl to Indian pearl merchants present for the lucrative season. Local merchants (*tawaeesh*) made no distinction between pearls and seed pearls, which were divided up by size and quality alone. The traditional tools used by the *tawaeesh* for this operation were graded sieves, scales and magnifying glasses. Pearls were stored in rain-water to remove the greenish tinge which often stains freshly harvested pearls. They were then wrapped in red cloth, sorted by size, weight and quality.

The term *ikhluwi* indicated a system in which the crew and the *nukhada* shared all the net profit of the season, distributed in a set manner depending on the type of work each individual performed. A*mil* denoted a system whereby the boat was owned and fitted out by an entrepreneur who was entitled to a major part of the proceeds at the end of the season, leaving the rest to be divided among the crew. The *amil*, a system originally particular to sheikhdoms other than that of Abu Dhabi, was probably widely applicable at the end of the century. It originally arose because pearlers, who belonged to different tribes and did not own date gardens, were not in a position to stock a pearling boat with the necessities so readily available to those closely related tribal groups that did have these assets. However, as the market for pearls expanded and surplus funds became available, the life of the versatile Abu Dhabi tribesman took on a more specialised nature. Whereas the tribal pearling co-operative had previously earned only enough to subsist, suddenly there was excess money available. Some utilised their share to buy more camels, others added to their date gardens, both groups paying labourers to take care

Opposite: *the shoreline of Abu Dhabi in the early 1960s*

of their property in their absence. Still others invested in the pearling industry so that in the end most boats were owned by individuals who finally took up residence in Abu Dhabi in the winter, living off their pearl earnings. Eventually entrepreneurs dominated the industry in Abu Dhabi, as they had already done for some time in other areas. Sub-tribes of the Bani Yas confederation such as the Rumaithat and Qubaisat settled the coastal islands and increased the population of Dubai and Abu Dhabi. The specialisation that evolved in these pearling communities meant that much of the egalitarian nature of the tribal society was replaced by a wage-earning system. This degree of specialisation was to be the downfall of these businessmen and indeed all those who depended on the pearling industry. Frauke Heard-Bey remarks that 'by contrast, the way of life of the tribal population in Abu Dhabi was not affected so radically by the decline of the pearling industry, because the families who had retained their roots in the desert concentrated again on utilising its resources.'

Boat–building

The earliest ships of the Muslim Arabs seem to have been relatively small craft, though information on the subject is scant. There was at first no native Islamic navy to complement the Muslim armies, though the Muslims must have inherited the powerful Sasanid navy and dock facilities after conquering this power on dry land. The Rightly-Guided Caliphs, coming as they did from the land-locked cities of the Hejaz, are said to have refused permission for troops to be transported by sea, such was their mistrust of the latter, the crossing from Julfar to the southern Iranian coast in 637 AD being a rare exception. The first Muslim General to flout this advice, creating a navy which was soon to dominate the Mediterranean as well as the seas around Arabia, was Mu'awiyyah, significantly their successor and founder of the Omayyad dynasty.

The absence of a navy did not signify any lack of maritime prowess. The Arabs were skilful sailors and had already developed the triangular lateen sail, enabling a ship to sail far closer to the wind than did the square sails used in the Mediterranean and northern seas. This sail was quickly copied and adapted by the Byzantines and Europeans after the penetration of the Mediterranean by Arab ships in the seventh century.

Apart from the lateen sail, the Arabs had another major contribution
to make in the art of seamanship. The Arabs of the Gulf developed their
own system of navigation based on astronomy, absorbing and in many
cases surpassing the work of the Chinese and Greek scholars in this field
and setting down their knowledge in navigational treatises, of which that
of Ahmed ibn Majid of Julfar is deservedly the most famous. Ibn Majid
knew all about the astrolabe and magnetic compass, but he preferred
to use the instruments known as *kashaba*, hand-held wooden sighting
instruments designed primarily to determine one's position by taking
a fix on the Pole Star relative to the horizon. This was ideal in the generally
cloudless skies of the Arabian Gulf, Red Sea and Indian Ocean.

When pearling was at its climax, the most important manufacturing
industry of the southern Gulf was boat-building. But, surprisingly, the
construction of *dhows* is still very much a living tradition in the Emirates
with at least as many traditional craft being constructed now as at the
beginning of the century. At that time Umm al-Qaiwain was an important
boat-building centre; about 20 boats were built there per year while
only approximately 10 were fashioned in Dubai. Today Ajman has the
Weaving a largest *dhow* building yard on the coast. Teak (*saj*) for planking, and for
fishing net. the keel, stem, stern and masts of the larger boats has traditionally been

imported from India; *mit* for the naturally grown crooks used to form ribs and knees from India, Somalia, Iran, and Iraq; rope from Zanzibar and the sail canvas from Bahrain or Kuwait, although some was made locally. Mango was also imported from India to make the smaller boats and dug-outs (*huri*). Only the *shashah*, built usually by its user, was made entirely from parts of the local date palm.

The *dhow* shipyards in the Emirates nurture this ancient boat-building tradition, using the same basic materials and tools to fashion elegant craft. Shell construction involving the fitting of planks first and ribs later is the usual system employed in *dhow* construction, contrasting with the European method of forming a skeleton of ribs prior to planking. Boats are all carvel-built with planks laid edge to edge; hundreds, sometimes thousands, of holes are hand-drilled to avoid splitting the wood and long thin nails, wrapped in oiled fibre, are driven through to secure the planks

to the frames. All the construction work is carried out without the aid of plans and drawings, measurements being made solely by eye and experience; templates are, however, used to shape the hull planking. Although it appears that accuracy depends solely on the instinct of the boat-builders, in fact a highly experienced master-craftsman (*ustadh*) usually oversees the calculations. The tools used in building boats, from the smallest to the largest, are very simple. Hammer, saw, adze, bow-drill, chisel, plane and caulking iron are, amazingly, all that is required to produce such a sophisticated and graceful end-product. The building of a large vessel could take anything up to ten months, while a smaller one – a *shu'i* for instance – would be finished in one to four months.

However, construction of Arab craft in the pre-Portuguese era differed somewhat from the modern form. Three distinctive features epitomised the *dhows* of this early period: coconut or palm-frond fibre rather than nails was used to sew the planks of the hull together; the hull shape was double-ended as opposed to square-sterned; and the sails had a fore-and-aft rather than square-rigged arrangement. All three features can be found on the east coast but, except in the Omani sewn *sambuq*, never in the one boat.

The famous 'Hariri' print (1237) is one of the few surviving representations of a medieval Arab ship before European influences brought changes. Their technical characteristics and relatively shallow draught meant that the traditional Arab ship was ideal for negotiating the treacherous coral reefs and sand-banks of the shallow Gulf waters. Stitched hulls appear also to have made the vessels more flexible, capable of standing the shock of being landed straight onto beaches in heavy surf. A disadvantage was their tendency to ship water, hence the depiction of the sailors bailing out water in the print. Oil, preferably shark-oil, was used in an attempt to prevent this by sealing up the cracks between the planks.

Arab trading ship. Maqamat of al-Hariri, Baghdad, 1237.

European influence over the centuries has given rise to a whole selection of *dhows* with square sterns; but the double-ended form persists in the *boum* and *badan* among others. The lateen sail remained unchanged, however the nailing of planks together has supplanted the less robust method of sewing.

Different types of vessel falling under the collective western title of *dhow* are individually named according to their particular hull shape. *Baghlah, boum, sambuq, shu'i, batil, baggarah* and *jalibut* and, to a lesser extent, the *huri* and *shashah* were all common in the Gulf at one stage or another. Varieties on which it is inconvenient or impossible to modify hulls to accommodate engines have, by and large, fallen into disuse and are no longer being built except for museum purposes. Sterns of all suitable types have been adapted and ribs extended to make way for modern engines, and outboard motors are now fitted on large numbers of dug-outs or *huris* and other fishing craft. Sometimes, however, one can observe a new functional and streamlined hull form, not corresponding to any traditional classification, developed specifically to accommodate an engine.

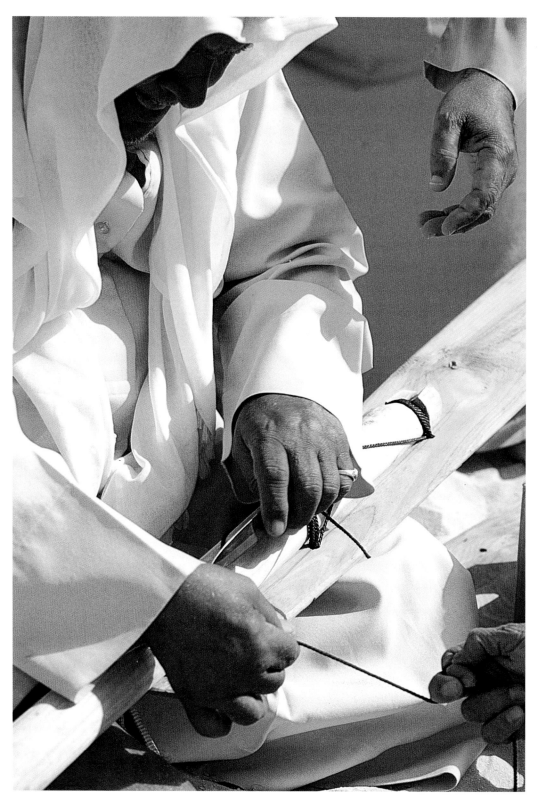

The Waves of Time

The double-ended *boum* is now the largest of all Arab vessels in the
Gulf, attaining a length anywhere between 15 and 37 metres. Easily
distinguishable by its high, straight stem-post, built out into a kind of
planked bowsprit decorated with a simple design in black and white,
it has superseded the ornately decorated square-sterned, high-
pooped *baghlah* as a trading vessel. The *boum* can be seen in great
numbers jostling for space at the quays of Dubai, laden with an eclectic
selection of goods from many different countries. The *sambuq*, boasting
an infinite variety of sizes, used to be one of the most common Arab

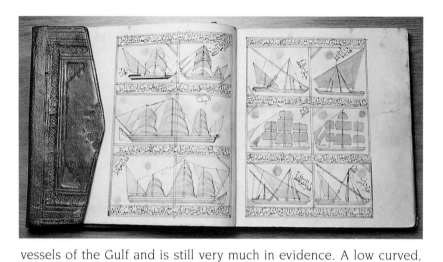

vessels of the Gulf and is still very much in evidence. A low curved, scimitar-shaped stem piece and high square stern lend elegance and grace to the lines of this useful boat. The length of the stem piece underwater and the resulting short keel allowed for easy manoeuvrability on the sand banks, making this a most popular pearling vessel but it was, and still is, used for trading and fishing purposes. *Shu'i*, basically small *sambuks*, rarely over 15 tons, but sporting a straight as opposed to curved stem piece are commonly used as fishing vessels. *Shashah*, on the other hand, are a totally different class of craft needing little skill and experience to build. Small (about 3 metres) and basic, they are made of date palm sticks tied with coir to form a point at bow and stern. Palm bark, coconut fibre and the bulbous ends of palm branches, packed into the bottom of the boat under a makeshift decking, lend buoyancy so that the boat lies flat on the water like a raft. Polystyrene is now favoured as a method of providing buoyancy and the substitution of nylon thread for coir has given greater strength to these fragile but flexible craft. It is precisely this flexibility that enables the *shashah* to withstand the pounding surf common on the east coast where they were once so popular.

Launching a shashah.

The traditional boat-building yards of Abu Dhabi, flanked by the modern marine club and marina adjacent to the Intercontinental hotel, provide the visitor with a unique image of a sea-faring past linked to the modern era. Everything necessary for the boat-building and fishing industry is fabricated here. Imported teak planks are cut on ancient band saws; iron nails forged at a makeshift foundry; anchors, fish traps and boats of every description all take shape under the careful eye of skilled craftsmen.

The Waves of Time

Charting UAE Waters

Andrew David

ALTHOUGH THE GENERAL OUTLINE of the Gulf was known to Arab scholars from an early date, European cartographers remained largely ignorant of the area as can be seen from a depiction of the Gulf in *The Boke of Idrogaphy*, the world atlas presented to King Henry VIII by the Dieppe cartographer Jean Rotz in 1542. When John Thornton published his chart 'Sinus Persicus' in *The English Pilot: The Third Book* in 1703 it contained a little more information, but this was entirely confined to the northeastern side of the Gulf with virtually no information at all about the coast and islands now comprising the United Arab Emirates. In 1709 a portolan chart of the Gulf drawn by John Friend of the Drapers' Company School contains very much the same information, but depicts in addition the factories of the European nations trading in the Gulf at this time including 'The City' (Basra), which was the British factory. Thus when Alexander Dalrymple began publishing a series of charts of the Gulf in 1786, the main emphasis was on charts suitable for ships trading between Bombay and Basra with no detail of any consequence on the coast of the UAE. Dalrymple's first chart of the Gulf merely reproduced Thornton's chart of the Gulf from his 1703 atlas and, on the same sheet, a similar chart from the 1716 atlas of his successor Samuel Thornton. Dalrymple also reproduced John Friend's 1709 chart

The Waves of Time

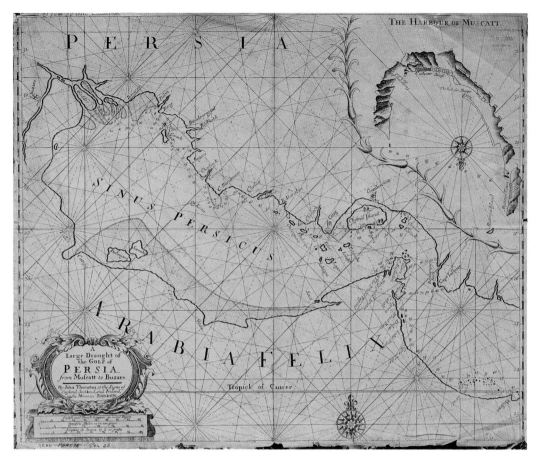

of the Gulf in 1787. A detailed survey of the Gulf carried out by John McCluer between 1785 and 1787, which Dalrymple published in 1788, did not even cover the UAE. There was no incentive for the British to examine the western part of the Gulf's southern shores because there appeared to be little in the way of trading possibilities, while the numerous islands, sandbanks and shoals rendered the area difficult to approach. Further north-eastwards, beyond Dubai, the inhabitants of the coastal settlements were viewed, with good cause, as being unfriendly to European shipping. Indeed it was as a result of a number of attacks by Qasimi vessels, principally based in Ras al-Khaimah, that British warships arrived in UAE waters. The attacks led the British to dub the area the 'Pirate Coast', although the present Ruler of Sharjah, Dr Sheikh Sultan bin Mohammed Al Qasimi, has convincingly argued that the reason for the conflict was more a matter of rivalry between the British and Qawasim over the important commercial shipping route through the mouth of the Gulf. During these operations the *Minerva*,

John Thornton's chart of the Arabian Gulf and its approaches was first published in 1703.

Capture of the Piratical Ship Minerva, by the Prince of Wales Schooner and boats of th... **538 FOLIO**

A naval artist's rendering of the scene off Ras al-Khaimah in 1809 when the schooner Prince of Wales, *together with other boats, bombarded the fort and sank vessels in the harbour.*

which had been captured by the Qawasim (referred to by the British as the Jonasmees), was recaptured in November 1809 and set on fire in front of Ras al-Khaimah by the schooner *Prince of Wales*, assisted by boats from the *Chiffone* and *Caroline*. Similar action led to the capture on 3 January 1810 of the fort at Shinas, just south of the present border between the UAE and Oman, by troops commanded by Lieutenant Colonel Smith, in which the *Chiffone* Captain, John Wainwright, appears to have taken part. During his time in the Gulf, Wainwright acquired a great deal of hydrographic information which he forwarded to the Admiralty, including detailed sailing directions and a number of surveys and views. According to Wainwright, the fear of attack had hitherto prevented a complete survey of the Gulf being undertaken:

but it is devotedly to be wished that so great an acquisition to Navigators as a correct chart will be made by the Directors of the Indian Government. The chart by McCluer is the best extant, but it is erroneous in the configuration of the coast.

Rumps [Rams] a Piratical Port SW'ward of Cape Musseldom [Ras Musandam], is in about latitude of 25. 53. N. Here the Mountains retire inland, and the waters begin to Shoal. The Creek of Rumps from its difficulty of approach in consequence of a Bar on which the Surf breaks heavily forms a good retreat . . . I annexe an eye draught which I made of it.

The Waves of Time

1810   Shinaus fort on the North East Coast of Arabia, taken by storm by the British forces, under Lieut. Colonel Smith, January 3rd 1810.   V 11537 FOLIO A

Unfortunately neither Wainwright's eye draughts, as he described his hurried sketch surveys, nor his views have survived. Ras al-Khaimah, he continued,

> . . . is situated on a sandy Point projecting to the NE; the water here is very shallow, so much so that a frigate cannot lie within four miles of the town. The ground is bad for holding being chiefly sand and shells. The best anchorage is with the Point bearing SE in six fathoms.
>
> There is an extensive creek at the back of the Town the approach to which is very shoal as a spit of sand runs from the Point, and forms a Bar on which at Spring Tides (when the rise of water is about six feet) there is never more than eleven feet.

Wainwright also visited the Tunbs reporting that:

> The Great Tomb [Greater Tunb] is a level island about three miles long and two and a half broad, on it are a few trees, it may be seen from a frigate's deck five leagues . . . water is to be obtained from a well near a Banyan Tree some distance from the Beach at the western end.
>
> The Little Tomb [Lesser Tunb]- an island rather less than the Great Tomb, appears at first in Hummocks, is barren, and like the Great Tomb uninhabited.

The artist's caption to this painting reads: "Shinaus fort on the North East coast of Arabia taken by storm by the British forces, under Lieut. Colonel Smith, January 3rd 1810."

With regard to the southern shores of the Gulf, Wainwright reported that:

Sketch of the UAE coastline prepared when it was known to the British as "The Pirate Coast" – a description that has been convincingly contradicted by several recent reviews of the period.

From Rumps to Sharga [Sharjah] the coast is low and indifferently planted with Date Trees. Several Creeks indent this shore capable of affording protection to the vessels of the piratical tribe of Jonasmee [the Qawasim]. It is hazardous for Ships to approach when the NW wind prevails for fear of them being embayed, but no danger appears from Cape Musseldom to Aboo Heyle [Abu Hail], a line of nearly thirty leagues. From the last mentioned place the Land extending to Bahrein [Bahrain] is called by the Arabs the Coast of Danger. It is wholly unknown to Europeans and many shoals are said to lie off it, while the bottom in general is Coral and Sand. The Arabian Coast to Graine [Kuwait] (in Latitude 29⅞ 12. N) where it may be said nearly to end is much of the same character. Along its whole extent a valuable Pearl Fishery is carried on by the Arabs, which People have always blended with the practice of Piracy some addiction to commercial pursuits . . .

[In Sharjah the] piratical dows lie in a small lagoon to the westward of the Town. Along this coast a bank of sand is thrown up by the violence of the Sea, which makes a good parapet for the Arab Matchlock Men.

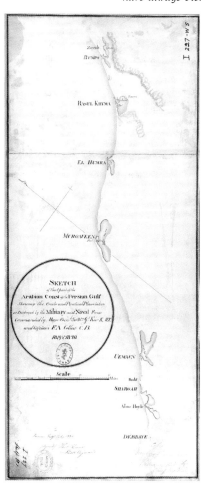

Attacks by the Qawasim continued in spite of the presence of British warships in the Gulf. Eventually a British expedition of over 3500 troops under the command of Sir William Grant Keir and Captain F.A. Collier, supported by the Navy, was sent against the Qawasim in 1819–20, during which eight villages on the coast were destroyed. Accompanying the expedition was Lieutenant Thomas Remon of the Engineers who produced a plan showing the locations of the villages that Keir attacked as well as individual plans of six of them. A plan of Rumps, drawn by J. Hawkins of the engineers, has also survived. The positions of the towers and forts destroyed during the expedition are depicted on the plans. As a result of this expedition treaties were signed in January 1820 between the British and the Arab Rulers, the beginning of what was to become the Trucial States (the present UAE).

Because of growing British interest in the Gulf, Captain Hurd, Hydrographer to the Admiralty, published the first British Admiralty chart of the Gulf on 21 September 1820, in which he incorporated the surveys and comments made by Wainwright, together with those of McCluer and others. Hurd's chart carries a legend at the western end of the coast of the UAE 'This part of the Coast is unknown', while offshore is charted the legend 'These eight Islands were seen, and their situation ascertained by the Hon[ble] Cap[t] Maude of H.M. Ship *Favourite* in 1816' and to seaward of these islands the legend 'The Great Pearl Bank'. The track of HMS *Hesper* in June and July 1813, with some soundings, is also shown on the chart between Dubai and a position some 70 miles south-west, with the legend along the adjacent coastline 'Low sandy Coast with Trees some Forts and small Villages interspersed'. On this chart the only part of the coast of the UAE which is depicted with any accuracy is from the Musandam Peninsula to the vicinity of Sharjah.

Plan of Murgaveen, prepared as part of the survey carried out in the 1820s by Lt. J.M. Guy and Lt. G.B. Brucks.

One of the most fruitful times to carry out hydrographic surveys is immediately after the conclusion of hostilities. Thus in 1820 the Bombay Marine gave instructions for a major survey of the Gulf to be carried out by Lieutenant John Michael Guy in the *Discovery* of 268 tons with Lieutenant George Barnes Brucks as his assistant in the *Psyche*. Guy started his survey the following year at Ras Musandam and by the end of 1822 he had reached Abu Dhabi. During these two years Guy had Lieutenant Robert Cogan as an additional assistant and together they surveyed Sir Bani Yas in 1822. By the end of 1824 Guy and Brucks had extended their survey as far as Ras Rakan at the head of the Qatar

Trigonometrical Plan of

ZIRCOOA ISLAND

in the Gulf of Persia

by

Lieut. J.M.Guy and G.B.Brucks

H.C.Marine

1823

Drawn by M.Houghton H.C.M.

Remarks

Latitude of the South point of the Island 24° 51' 44" North. Variation 3° 53' West.
Longitude of ditto 53° 13' 17" East. Soundings for low water, and in fath.

Chart of the UAE island now known as Zirku, based on a survey by Lt. J.M. Guy and Lt. G.B. Brucks.

Peninsula, and it thus seems likely that they completed the survey of the coast of the UAE and its outlying islands by the end of 1823. While Guy endeavoured to base his surveys on a system of triangulation, this was rarely possible as in places the coast is fringed with low and featureless islands up to 20 miles offshore, making triangulation impracticable. In addition, because of the difficult terrain, many of the bases on which his survey depended were measured by sound between the two ships rather than on shore. Survey marks such as poles and flags would also have been an obvious temptation to local tribesmen. Thus many of Guy's surveys were in fact running surveys, controlled where possible by astronomical observations both on board ship and on shore. Because refraction is a major factor in the Gulf, Guy always used an

The Waves of Time

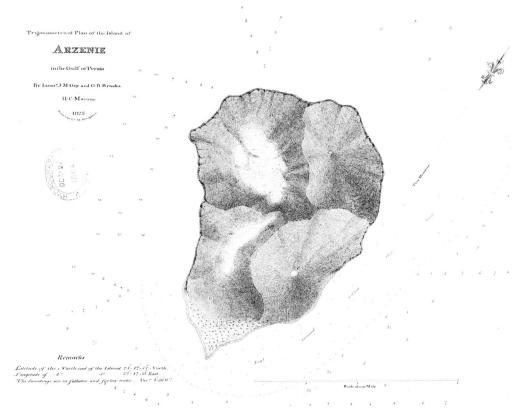

artificial horizon, in conjunction with a sextant on a stand, for his observations on shore since it was useless to observe with the natural horizon. An artificial horizon is simply a pool of mercury which naturally lies in a horizontal plane. In taking the altitude of the sun as it crosses the meridian at noon, in order to calculate latitude, the observèr measures, by sextant, the angle between the sun and its reflection in the mercury. The resulting angle is twice the true angle between the sun and the horizon. Since the greatest angle that can be measured by a sextant is 120 per cent, latitude cannot be obtained by this method if the sun's meridian altitude is greater than about 55 per cent. This probably limited the surveying season to the winter months, since when the sun crosses the celestial equator at the vernal equinox, its meridian altitude at noon in 24 per cent N, at the southern shores of the Gulf, would be 66 per cent. Guy's longitudes were obtained by chronometer measured from the meridian of the English factory at Bassadore (B_sa'_d_) on Kishma Island (Jazireh-ye Qeshm), whose longitude had been fixed by meridian distances from Bombay, which in those days was placed 7 miles too far to the east.

Survey of the UAE island now known as Arzanah, based on a survey by Lt. J.M. Guy and Lt. G.B. Brucks.

Southern shores of the Gulf as charted before Guy's survey (based on Hurd's 1820 chart).

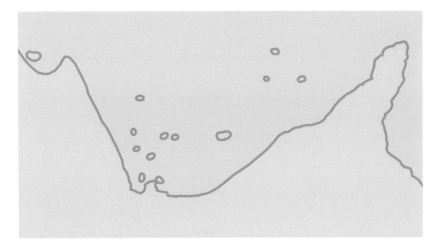

Guy had to return to Bassadore at intervals to check the errors of his chronometers and to obtain provisions. These were also obtained from time to time during the survey from the local Sheiks. At Shaum, [Sharm] for instance, 'The Sheik, and those under him, were very civil to the officers of the surveying vessels, and a constant supply was afforded of poultry, goats, milk, and butter, with a few vegetables, at a reasonable rate.' Similarly, at Ras al-Khaimah 'Supplies of bullocks,

Chart compiled after Guy's survey by Horsburgh in 1832.

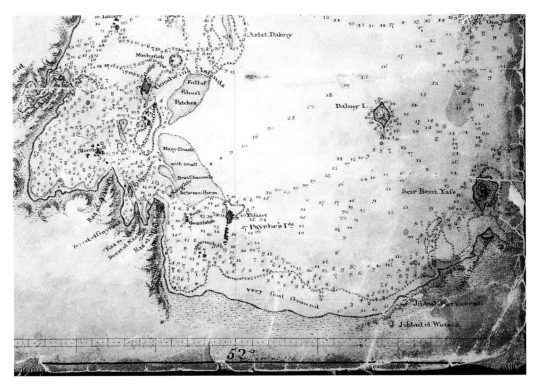

The Waves of Time

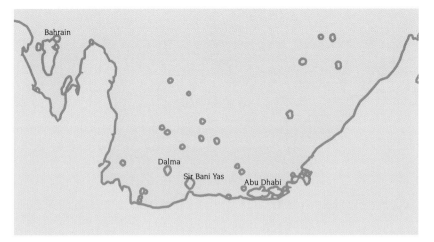

Southern shores of the Gulf as charted after Guy's survey (based on Horsburgh's 1832 chart).

fowls, butter, and vegetables, are procured at very reasonable rates and . . . no want of these articles was experienced on any part of what is generally termed the Pirate Coast . . . ' Guy may also have observed lunar distances to check the performances of his chronometers, a method in which the movement of the moon in the heavens was used to obtain Greenwich Mean Time. Soundings were obtained by lead line from which the height of the tide was subtracted to reduce them to a

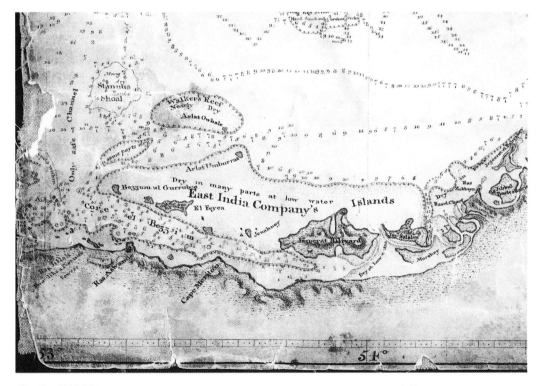

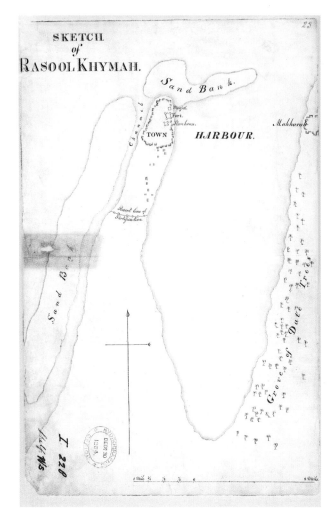

SKETCH
of
RASOOL KHYMAH.

Sand Bank.

Channel

Masjid.
Fort.
Storehouses.
TOWN   HARBOUR.   Makhara

Recent line of Fortification

Sand Bank

Sand Bank

Grove of Date Trees

I 220

DEC 30 1864

1 Mile ¾ ½ ¼ 0   2 Miles

Ras al-Khaimah.

low water datum. In some parts of Guy's survey there are numerous soundings, but in other parts there are large areas with few soundings or even no soundings at all, an inevitable result in a survey which was principally aimed at discovering the correct delineation of the coastline and the positions and extent of the off-lying islands. Guy was faced with the dilemma faced by all surveyors of his generation when surveying a completely unknown stretch of coastline. Such a survey is inevitably a compromise between absolute accuracy and completing the survey of a large extent of coastline to an acceptable degree of accuracy in a reasonable length of time. In such a survey it is inevitable that not all dangers will be discovered. In general, the coast is fringed by extensive areas of shallow water in which coral outcrops are not uncommon. These can be small in extent, rising steeply from the seabed, so that soundings give little indication of their proximity. If, in addition, they lack a covering of sand, the usual warning of lighter coloured water may be absent, making them particularly difficult to locate.

Guy's instructions were to survey the whole of the Gulf, but when he reached Khor Abdulla, at the head of the Gulf, his health gave way and Brucks took over the survey and we must rely on the latter's memoir, published in 1856, to learn about Guy's survey. In it Brucks wrote that Ras al-Khaimah, prior to the expedition of 1819–1820, was:

> . . . *surrounded on three sides with a wall, flanked with towers, and to the south-westward of the town had a further defence of strong square fort or Ghuree, and was at that time supposed to be defended by between six and seven thousand*

men, including the auxiliaries collected from the country round about, and about eighty boats of different size, from two hundred and fifty to forty or fifty tons, some mounting eight and ten guns. They also had about sixty or seventy pieces of Cannon, of various descriptions, but most of them would be considered unserviceable by Europeans. A number of their best boats were sent to Lingah and other friendly places, by which they escaped being destroyed, and are now employed with trade.

Brucks also commented on Sharjah and Abu Heyle (Abu Hail):

Shargah . . . is long and narrow and open: the defences are a fort a little inland, mounting six pieces of Cannon together with some detached towers. In case of alarm from an enemy, it is stockaded round with Date trees and wood sufficient for repelling the attack of Arabs, although of little service against regular troops . . . Shargah sends from three to four hundred boats of various sizes to the pearl fishery.
Aboo Heyle is a small village situated about three miles to the SW of Shargah, on the same creek with Khan village on the other bank. They jointly contain about two hundred and fifty inhabitants of various tribes, mostly fishermen, and are subject to Shargah

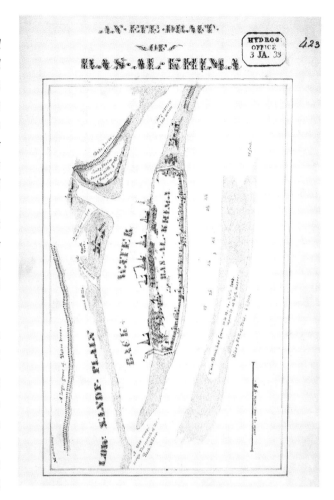

Ras al-Khaimah.

The survey conducted by Brucks went no further westward than Dubai along the coastline, although he also described all the islands that he and Guy surveyed. According to him Jezirat Arzanah was moderately elevated and about six and a half miles in circumference, while its south point, like most of the islands, was low and sheltered from the prevailing winds. Good anchorage could be found under the lee of the island, but there was no water. He considered that Jezirat Zarakkuh (Zirku) was

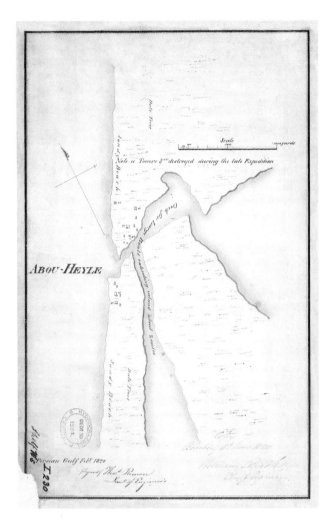

ABOU-HEYLE

the highest island off the south coast of the Gulf and that it afforded good anchorage under its lee, sheltered from the prevailing wind. It too had no water. Sheltered anchorage from northerly winds was essential for the safety of the two ships since in winter the *shamal* can blow at times with considerable violence.

The results of the surveys carried out by Guy and Brucks covering the waters of the UAE are given in a small scale chart, extending from the Musandam Peninsula to Khor Abdulla at the head of the Gulf, and nine large scale plans of off lying islands. On the completion of the survey in 1830 a small scale chart of the Gulf was drawn on two sheets, which James Horsburgh, Hydrographer to the East India Company, published on 1 January 1832, also in two sheets. The publication of this chart led to the withdrawal of the chart of the Gulf published by Hurd in 1820, which thus was in publication for a very short time. When the Admiralty took

A *twentieth century sketch of Ras al-Khaimah.*

The Waves of Time

over all charting responsibilities of the East India Company in 1861, Horsburgh's chart continued to be published by the Hydrographer of the Navy as charts 90 (a) and (b).

Following Guy's survey there were no further major surveys of the coastal waters of the UAE for over 100 years, although a number of minor surveys of small extent were carried out during this period. Perhaps the most significant of these were a survey of 'Part of the Great Tomb' by Lieutenant L.B. Haines in 1835-6, one of Jezirat-yer Sirri by Lieutenant Collingwood in 1857 and one of Abu Musa by Commander H.C. Somerville in 1911 and 1912. Guy's initial survey, completed by Brucks, continued to provide the basis of all knowledge of the hydrography of the southern Gulf until after the Second World War. Only then, with the commencement of major surveys that coincided with the beginning of offshore oil exploration, was the work of these early British surveyors finally superseded.

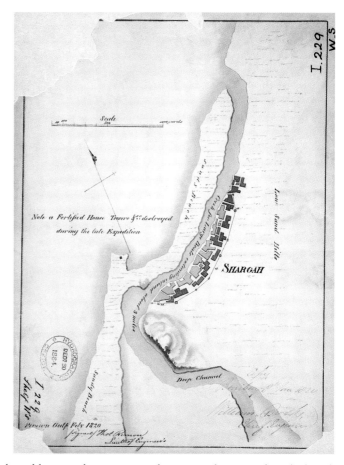

A *plan of Sharjah harbour drawn in* 1820.

A *twentieth century sketch of* Abu Dhabi.

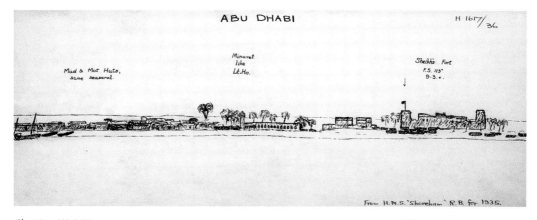

Harvesting the Sea

Simon Aspinall   THE UNITED ARAB EMIRATES possesses a coastline over 1400 kilometres in length including that of its numerous Arabian Gulf islands, many channels or *khors* and other indentations. The mainland coast inside the Arabian Gulf extends a straight line distance of approximately 450 kilometres, while the Gulf of Oman coast is approximately 80 kilometres in length. As a result of fluctuating sea levels, the coastline has changed substantially since prehistoric times. In particular, the formation of the *sabkha* salt flats, believed to have taken place around 2000 BC (4000 BP), has prograded and infilled an extensive area of coastal embayments and shallow lagoons along the Arabian Gulf coast, notably north-east and to the west of the island of Abu Dhabi. The shallow gradient of the seabed has meant that, since the end of the flooding of the Arabian Gulf following the retreat of the last great Ice Age, approximately 10,000 years ago, even a minor rise or fall would result, respectively, in an extensive incursion or retreat.

The coast of the UAE presents a variety of littoral habitats, with the largely unbroken belt of *sabkha*, the largest active example of its kind in the world, penetrating as much as 20–30 kilometres inland from the present-day coastline west of Abu Dhabi for much of the distance to the border with the Kingdom of Saudi Arabia. It is punctuated only by

the occasional rocky headland or peninsula, these outcrops most often being of Miocene or Plio-Pleistocene age. Along the western border with Saudi Arabia, the great Sabkhat Matti extends over 100 kilometres inland. Numerous low-lying inshore islands exist now, as indeed they have done for several thousand years, formed, for the most part, by a dissection of a once intact *sabkha*. The setting is much the same north-east of Abu Dhabi to the border with Dubai between Ras Ghanadha and Jebel Ali. Thereafter an exposed shoreline, predominantly sandy, prevails, interrupted by the peculiar low-energy and often biologically rich *khors* or ʿkhawrsʾ (mostly shaped or modified by dredging today) such as at Khor Dubai, Ajman's Khor Zawra and Khor al-Beidah and al-Jazirah, Khor in Umm al-Qaiwain and Ras al-Khaimah respectively.

On the UAE's East Coast, either the mountains come down to the shores of what is known as the Gulf of Oman, or there is a narrow tree-studded alluvial foreland. Many coastal fishing villages and hamlets in the mouths of the mountain *wadis* remain unchanged by the recent modernisation seen elsewhere in the country. Small fishing boats are still launched from the beach today, although some ports have grown up, mostly catering for the handling of oil or container cargoes.

Mangroves, once more widely distributed, can be found at Khor Kalba on the East Coast, and in sheltered waters along the Arabian Gulf coast. The principal areas of mangrove today are around Dhabbiyah, Abu Dhabi island and north to Ras Ghanadha, Khor al-Beidah, at Dhayah/Rams in Ras

The Waves of Time

al-Khaimah and at Khor Kalba on the East Coast in Sharjah Emirate. A single species, *Avicennia marina* (the black mangrove), occurs in the Gulf, its most northerly occurrence world-wide, the limiting factor being winter temperature.

Many coral-fringed offshore islands exist, a number being the higher parts of diapiric extrusions, formed by salt deposits migrating (flowing) under pressure, which have then punched their way to the surface along lines of weakness, exemplified perhaps by the island of Qarnein, which takes its name from the two horns ('*ithnayn*' and '*carn*') which tower skywards to over 50 metres on the otherwise low, flat, three

Dugong grazing on the seabed.

kilometre-long island. Sir Bani Yas, Zirku, Sir Abu Nu'air and Delma are four other such, far larger, salt-dome islands, while on the mainland, Jebel Dhanna is similarly formed. A number of these islands have a long history of human occupation from the Late Stone Age, around 7000 BP onwards. Qarnein, much further offshore and around 120 kilometres out into the Gulf, appears to have been used more sporadically although it has yielded pottery from the early first millennium AD, providing evidence of maritime commerce through the Gulf.

Marine life is abundant in the Arabian Gulf, despite the particularly high water temperatures in summer and resulting high salinity, which is presumably responsible for reducing the diversity of species found (compared to other tropical waters, such as the Red Sea), but which has little effect on the overall biomass. Coral development, along with its associated plant and animal communities, occurs to within a few metres of the shore, more so on the East Coast than within the Arabian Gulf; while another important ecosytem is the extensive seagrass beds of the shallow shoals and inshore leads. Hawksbill turtle (*Eretmochelys imbricata*) and green turtles (*Chelonia mydas*) feed extensively in both coral and seagrass locations, in some areas at extremely high densities, while egg-laying takes place on a few of the outer islands and, to a lessening amount, on selected mainland beaches. The three metre-long dugong, or seacow (*Dugong dugon*), grazes the seagrass beds in western Abu Dhabi and possibly still in Umm al-Qaiwain. Cetaceans also abound, the two commonest species being bottle-nosed dolphin (*Tursiops truncatus*) and Indo-Pacific humpback dolphin (*Sousa sinensis*), the latter common inshore.

As a result of recent surveys it is now known that tens of thousands of pairs of several species of tern nest annually on the islands in summer, a small number of islands supporting the bulk of their populations. Conversely, the Socotra cormorant (*Phalacrocorax nigrogularis*) breeds in late autumn and winter, once again in vast colonies on certain islands. The UAE population of this endemic Arabian species is estimated to number around 200,000 individuals, although it was definitely larger in the past.

Use by the UAE's inhabitants of available resources has never been restricted to food. Naturally occurring organic and inorganic materials have also been used for construction purposes, for ornamentation or decoration, as medicines and for ritual performance, although little is known of the last. Patterns of subsistence, levels of technology reached and economic development through time can be deduced to some extent.

The long history of occupation and utilisation of natural resources along the coast and on the islands of the UAE has been unearthed only relatively recently through archaeological excavation. The population of the country has clearly looked to the sea and its bountiful resources from the very earliest of times, whereas the interior of the country would have been, to some extent, a more testing environment in which to live. Sweet water to nurture farming activities was a precious commodity drawn from hand-dug wells. The human population was, furthermore, necessarily transient

Cuttlefish (Sepia) courting.

or nomadic until relatively recently, with rather few permanent settlements existing (some being occupied seasonally), invariably located where fresh water could be obtained. Trade with northern Gulf ports, with Basra (Iraq) and Bandar Abbas (Iran) amongst others brought in goods from as far afield as China, some commodities in substantial quantities, to these coastal communities.

Man has exploited the sea in the southern Gulf region for over 7000 years. Collection of shellfish and crustacea (mainly crabs), perhaps seasonal and probably undertaken daily to ensure freshness, would certainly have been an easily accomplished task, gathering being by hand or with a trident. There is extensive evidence for large-scale harvesting, with accumulations of discarded shells forming significant mounds and in some instances even forming a firm base on which habitations or shelters were then built. Such middens have been located along much of the country's coastline, and it is through the excavation of some of them that early dietary preferences have been partially determined.

Bottlenosed dolphin (Tursiops truncatus).

One hundred and fifteen species of mollusc (49 bivalves & 63 gastropods) have been listed from excavations in the UAE. Despite the high diversity of species found, however, just three predominate, a bivalve and two gastropods, respectively, *Pinctada radiata*, the pearl oyster, and *Hexaplex kuesterianus* and *Terebralia palustris*, although all three do not necessarily co-occur at the same time or place. Oysters were collected by divers primarily during spring and summer as food, from at least 4000 BP, and in the quest for pearls (*lulu*) from the southern Gulf's innumerable *fasht* (oyster-beds).

Molluscs were certainly taken as food, but perhaps also used as fishing bait. Unburnt shells may indicate boiling of the catch, rather than cooking in a fire, although presumably some may have been eaten raw. The larger middens, which can be 2–3 three metres high and 6–8 metres across would have taken decades or even centuries to amass.

Cephalopods, a branch of the phylum *Mollusca* (including squids and octopi), may have provided a minor component of an ancestral diet, cuttlefish plates having been found, albeit sparingly, in some excavations and more recent household detritus, although these were possibly nothing more than a by-catch. Squid is certainly popular today.

Shells were used variously as ornamentation, as containers, and for preparation of dye or pigments as, for example, of the cuprous mineral

Mangroves fringe many of the islands.

atacamite which was used for eye-makeup. Worked shells were pierced and used as buttons and beads while pearls (for jewellery and possibly as a form of currency) have been collected since at least the Late Stone Age.

The mangrove is an especially valuable resource with multiple uses. These include charcoal production for cooking and smelting, timber for house construction and boat-building, leaves for tanning and the foliage as browse for camels. Camels are still able to graze in some mangrove areas, most notably that at Khor Kalba and on Jubayl near Abu Dhabi. The collection of honey from natural combs and from purpose-built hives in the mangroves continues, and is presumably an occupation of some antiquity.

Much other food can also be found in and around mangal woodland, although harvesting is now primarily a recreational pursuit. Swimming crabs (*Portunidae*), various other crab species and molluscs, in particular the mud-dwelling *Terebralia*, now much rarer than in the past, would have been gathered en masse, while fish were netted, speared and trapped. Waterfowl will have been brought down on occasion.

In coastal areas, the Salicornias, salad plants found in saltmarsh communities, are still consumed in small quantities and may have been of greater importance in the past. More popular and still eagerly sought along the coast/littoral zone in winter is the subterranean fungus known as '*faqah*,' or the desert truffle.

Coral and '*faroush*' (*farush*) or beach rock, a lithified carbonate deposit, is a common building material, whether for habitation, storm shelters for humans or animals, pens, corrals or graves. *Faroush* has the added advantage of breaking or being broken easily into flat relatively lightweight slabs. Both crude and more sophisticated buildings, constructed from faced blocks of coral were certainly being built several centuries ago, although few remain intact today. The now largely-abandoned fishing and pearling village of Jazirat al-Hamra, on the coast south of Ras al-Khaimah, offers useful visual evidence of how such coral-built structures gradually disintegrate over time, leaving little more than powdered rubble. Stone-built fish traps in shallow coastal waters have also been used for centuries, while the construction of artificial reefs, by dropping or sinking rocks and other materials onto an otherwise sandy seabed may be another long-practised management technique, which is continued today.

Harvesting of fish from the UAE's waters has a major role in the economy, both for subsistence and for trade. The practice of splitting and drying fish (small fish e.g. *jashr* (anchovies) or *uma* (sardines) were dried whole, spread out on the ground), and of salting the largest specimens allowed the provision of this valuable commodity to the population of the hinterland, as far inland as the former oasis town of Al-Ain, since grown into a flourishing city, or to the Liwa on the fringes of the Empty Quarter. Some fishmeal was used as camel fodder or as fertiliser, for example, silversides in vegetable gardens.

Salt was always an important commodity and, having an additional value as a preservative for fresh-caught fish destined for markets in the inland oases, it was harvested through the simple technology of trapping seawater and allowing it to evaporate in the sun. The last traces of this rudimentary industry lasted until very recently, as in Ajman.

Investigation of middens has shown that fishery methods may have varied. On Sir Bani Yas, only 8 kilometres offshore, for example, midden deposits have yielded bones of the Sparidae or seabream family, and the fishery was clearly therefore an inshore one. Small gauge nets or baskets rather than hooks may have been used. Further offshore on the island of Dalma, however, midden deposits have revealed a preference for the hamour or brown-spotted grouper (*Epinephilus tauvina*). These would have to have been hooked or caught in larger traps, although some local fishermen with a particularly good knowledge of the waters developed a practice of diving and extricating the fish from its reef lair by hand. Evidence from a 6000 year old midden on Dalma

Gargour traps ready for setting.

The Waves of Time

has suggested that hamour may then have attained a length of up to 1.5 metres, a size now virtually unknown, perhaps as a result of over-fishing. Traditional fishing methods continue today. *Hadra* are deceptively simple fence traps constructed perpendicularly out from the shore, which shepherd fish into a baffled heart-shaped maze where they are left as the tide recedes. They are in use both along the Gulf's mainland coast and on inshore islands. *Gargour* traps, another ingenious device for trapping fish unharmed, originally made of plant materials, such as palmleaf stems and blades, but now of wire, are igloo-shaped domes, weighted to the seabed with rocks or cement and baited with fresh or putrescent fish which entices a variety of fish to enter through a one-way funnel-like opening. Return passage is not possible for larger fish, due to the progressive inward narrowing. These traps are deployed from boats, being hauled back to surface for emptying

and baiting once more. Fishermen today target many different species, pre-eminent amongst which are *safi* (rabbit fish), *shari* (emperor), kingfish, *hamra* (red snapper), *jersh* (jacks), *gobab* (tuna) and groupers as well as shrimps and *cigales* (crayfish). Those species suitable for commercial fish farming, such as *safi* and shrimps, are increasingly being raised, with considerable success. *Zubedi* (silver pomfret) is one of the most expensive fishes in the *soukh*.

Commercial export of fish and fish products is also probably of long tradition, in particular the export of dried shark fins, still shipped in some quantities to Far Eastern markets. Shark oil is highly regarded as a health giver, although little oil is produced locally. The oil, according to Elders, is used as a condiment and, previously, as a sealant for boats.

Turtle eggs and turtle meat have long been exploited. In recent years, this has been banned under the UAE's increasingly extensive portfolio of environmental protection legislation, although some infringement continues. Fishing communities harpooned turtles and collected the newly-laid eggs from mainland and island breeding sites. Green turtles predominated in catches. Hawksbill, found further offshore in the main, were less frequently taken, although the eggs would have been gathered from any nest-pit encountered. Loggerhead turtle (*Caretta caretta*)may also have been hunted; scarce today, it has possibly always been so. Perhaps strangely, no evidence of tortoiseshell, i.e. worked turtle carapace, has been reported from archaeological sites. Such carapaces doubtless served as storage containers.

Crab plovers at
Khor al Baidah,
UAE.

Seabirds undoubtedly provided an extremely valuable source of food, adding to the already wide variety of animals exploited. In the summer months nesting colonies of terns, especially bridled tern (*Sterna anaethetus*), white-cheeked tern (*S. repressa*) and lesser-crested tern (*S. bengalensis*), and sooty gulls (*Larus hemprichii*) were visited by egg-collecting parties and with many thousands of birds nesting close together the harvesting job could be accomplished over a matter of just a few days. Replacement clutches of some species might also have been gathered, but obviously at a sustainable level. It is probable that the eggs were merely consumed as required by fishing or pearling parties coming ashore on the islands during the long pearling seasons in spring and summer.

The scarce crab plover (*Dromas ardeola*) lays an egg which is large in proportion to its size, larger than a hen's egg and these, together with the nestlings, which were located in a chamber at the end of a 2–3 metre-long underground burrow, excavated by the bird itself on sandbanks close to crab-filled mangroves, were eagerly collected. Only two colonies are known to exist on the western shore of the Gulf, and chicks and eggs were certainly collected until very recently from at least one of these colonies, providing a further supplement to what must often have been a fairly unvaried diet.

Another bird of economic significance was the Socotra cormorant (*Phalacrocorax nigrogularis*) which breeds through the autumn and winter period on remote offshore islands, importantly at a time when other nesting seabirds were unobtainable. Both its eggs and its nestlings were collected.

According to the Arab traveller and historian Al Idrisi, guano, unquestionably produced by the Socotra cormorant, was collected as a fertiliser and was exported to Basra, in Iraq, in the thirteenth century AD for use as fertiliser on vines and palm trees. A licence to collect guano from the islet of Mahamalliyah, an important roost site in the far west of Abu Dhabi, was still in operation as recently as 50 years ago.

Dugong, weighing in at up to a hefty 500 kilograms, would have represented a protein source well worth hunting. The dried meat was and still is particularly valued as food. The herds have been reduced in number and, as with turtles, legal protection is now in force. It might have been expected that the carcass would have been put to a multitude of other uses (as a skin for waterproof roofing perhaps, or as a hull for a coracle-like boat) but no documentary or other source provides any supporting evidence. Surprisingly, no carved or etched dugong tusk has ever been reported, although one suggested and plausible possibility, in the absence of antler as was used elsewhere, for example in Europe and North America, was the use of the tusks as a soft hammer to pressure flake the edges of 'bifacial' flint or chert tools such as spears and arrowheads during the Late Stone Age. A diverse stone toolkit was employed, blades, knives, drills and tanged points for example, even if the raw materials themselves were not available locally but had to be imported.

Dugong were obviously hunted deliberately. Butchered remains, sometimes of many individuals, show such hunts to have been well organised, with animals being harpooned in the shallow waters of Abu Dhabi Emirate, Umm al-Qaiwain and elsewhere. Meat was dried in the sun on racks and transported to inland markets as well as being consumed by the coastal-dwelling populace. In comparison, the capture of cetaceans seems to have been, at best, an opportunistic event. Bones of bottle-nosed dolphins, humpback dolphins and finless porpoise *Neophocoena phocoenoides* have turned up in some sites (along with skeletal remains of miscellaneous waterbirds), these mostly being Late Islamic in age. There is occasional evidence, as, for example, in a fishing village on Merawah, of whalebones being used for construction, although perhaps none were ever deliberately hunted or netted. Capture, in any case, would have been an altogether more difficult task than with dugong which could be 'cornered' in shallow leads. The skin of whales was used

to make water containers, while the oil from the whale's blubber was used for the waterproofing of boats and also as a fuel for lamps (per Khadim Rumaithi).

Finally, another unusual marine resource collected by the people of the Emirates from shallow offshore waters was water itself – fresh water. In some areas offshore, underground aquifers carrying fresh water from the Hajar Mountains inland percolated upwards to the seabed. Although these were never as plentiful as those off the coast of Bahrain or Qatar, further up the Arabian Gulf, some were certainly utilised. Off the island of Bazm al-Gharbi, west of Abu Dhabi, for example, local fishermen still point out the former site of one such spring, with tracks through the coral made by donkeys on their way to the spring and a scatter of pottery from broken storage vessels still visible. It has been said that pearl divers may also have collected potable water from these submarine springs.

On the Gulf islands and perhaps on the mainland too, rainwater was channelled into and stored in cisterns (or natural lowpoints), while horizontally hung sails were also used to take advantage of occasional downpours which would have been seen approaching from the north.

The historical record of the significance of marine resources to the human populace of what is now the United Arab Emirates is gradually unfolding. Traditional patterns of harvesting and consumption from the marine environment have been a key part of the way of life of the country's people, and in some parts of the country or amongst the older generation, more so than might be imagined, this former reliance is still part of everyday life.

New Wealth from the Sea

Stephen Howarth

JUST A FEW DECADES AGO, no one could have imagined that the seven members of the United Arab Emirates would ever enjoy the wealth that they do today. The main source of that wealth is oil and gas, and the offshore industry is the newest version of the UAE's oldest tradition: the use of the sea as a source of prosperity. Offshore oil and gas are the latest manifestations of the UAE's marine heritage. The modern focus on oil and gas has altered much in the Emirates: most vividly and visibly, the seascape and landscape. Yet not everything has changed. The physical alterations are dramatic, but underlying and pervading these alterations there is, even more remarkably, a great spiritual continuity.

The UAE's links with the sea are ancient and intimate. Ever since the first human settlements over 7000 years ago, the waters of the Arabian Gulf and the Arabian Sea have played an indispensable part in the life of the people, both as a source of food and a method of communication, trade and travel. For many centuries, the region's boatbuilders and seafarers were renowned for their skills in construction and navigation. Merchant vessels traded throughout the Gulf, all over the Indian Ocean and as far as China, but the region's most celebrated marine product was pearls, first known to have been collected at least 6000 years ago. They continued to be a highly significant source of

revenue right up to the twentieth century, and for many people, participation in the pearling industry made the difference between the barest subsistence and modest comfort.

Although the people of the Emirates, particularly those living on the coast, had long benefited from their involvement in the commerce of the Indian Ocean, the country itself apparently had little in the way of natural resources. Copper mining had commenced in the Hajar Mountains prior to 3000 BC, and had been a source of considerable revenue in the pre-historic period; thereafter it declined, although some mining continued until the sixteenth or seventeenth century AD.

As pearling slowly ceased to be supportive, oil seemed to hold out some hope as an alternative. People had known for thousands of years that petroleum (crude oil) existed in other parts of the Middle East. In some areas, like southern Iran, natural seepages had been big enough to have had various simple traditional uses. It was employed, for example, to caulk boats, while analysis of pottery found at the 2000 year old port of Ad Door, in Umm al-Qaiwain, has shown that some of the pots were waterproofed by treating them with bitumen, probably imported from an area of seepage in Iran.

Some evidence of oil on the Gulf coast of Arabia had always been apparent: sometimes streaks were seen on the sea, occasional lumps of tar (so heavy as to sink in water) were washed up on beaches. Such quantities were too small to be useful, even for caulking: indeed, the only oil traditionally used in Arab *dhows* was shark oil, as a pungent but effective preservative. Nevertheless, by the end of the 1930s it was virtually certain that petroleum must exist in the Emirates. Whether you looked east, north or west, oil had been found in every surrounding country: relatively far off in Iran (1908), Egypt (1913) and Iraq (1927), and very close to home in Bahrain (1932), Kuwait and Saudi Arabia (both 1938), and Qatar (1939). The Financial Times of London had already reported in 1936 that 'the rising importance of the Arabian Coast as a petroleum producer has been strikingly shown by Bahrain's appearance this year as an exporter of 250,000 tons from January to June.' With similar geology to that of Bahrain, the whole Arabian coast of the Gulf was under active exploration, and from 1937 to 1939 Sharjah, Dubai, Abu Dhabi, Ras al-Khaimah and Ajman in turn granted concessions to Petroleum Concessions Limited, the exploration arm of the Iraq Petroleum Company (IPC), a consortium comprising the major European and American international oil companies.

Almost immediately, the Second World War put a stop to exploration and condemned the Emirates to further years of poverty. Unproductive, barren, almost completely waterless and with their trade savagely diminished, their combined annual revenue at the time was barely half a million pounds sterling; and from a total population of no more than 180,000 strong, emigration was steady, with about 2000 people leaving every month to work in the oilfields of Kuwait, Qatar, Bahrain and Saudi Arabia. But not long after the war, far away in the Gulf of Mexico, there was a sensational development: a small American oil company drilled the world's first oil well out of sight of land, more than 16 kilometres from the coast in water 6 metres deep. The Arabian Gulf is shallow, nowhere more than 100 metres deep and on average just 25 metres. Suddenly people from the Emirates could gaze across its waters with renewed excitement and conjecture. Could it be that once again the sea might provide? The rise of the UAE since then has been one of the most astonishing stories in the history of the global oil business. Today it has the third largest proven recoverable reserves of oil in the world, constituting about 12 per cent of OPEC reserves and nearly 10 per cent of world reserves; only Saudi Arabia and Iraq have more. In proportion to its size, the UAE has more oil per hectare than anywhere else on earth; and it was not under the earth, but under the sea, that this phenomenal treasure was first discovered. Abu Dhabi granted its first post-war offshore concession in 1951. Although work commenced with high hopes, the results were extremely disappointing, and after a limited and unsuccessful exploring effort, the original concessionaire withdrew in 1953.

Commander Jacques-Yves Cousteau examines the navigational hazards of the area.

However, in 1954 Abu Dhabi Marine Areas Ltd (ADMA) was created by British Petroleum and the Companie Francises des Petroles (later TOTAL), and immediately received a concession on 19,000 square kilometres in the Gulf. ADMA proved to be the agent of change. Today it is commonplace for drilling operations to take place in water hundreds of metres deep, but when ADMA began work an operational depth of 20 metres was a real challenge. A team led by the French diver, Commander Jacques-Yves Cousteau (inventor of the aqualung, and then the greatest living authority on deep-sea diving), was engaged for preliminary exploration. In the early months of 1954, based in his 400- ton oceanographic research ship *Calypso*, the team covered 400 'stations' in 67 working days. The weather was unusually cold, the visibility both above and below water unusually bad, and the ship had to weather several storms; but these were perhaps the most valuable 67 days in the Emirates' history. Taking photographs and rock samples, the explorers described the seabed as looking much like the desert on shore: rolling plains, with very few cliffs or caverns. What they could not tell at first sight was whether the seabed's similarity to the desert continued underneath as well. Using gravimeters, they measured the magnetic strength of rock strata far below. The readings seemed promising enough to warrant a fuller seismic survey, and when the data had been analysed, a recommendation was made to drill a test well.

ADMA commissioned the construction of a drilling barge named *Adma Enterprise*, the first of its kind to be built in Europe. Displacing 4200 tons, the barge measured 60 metres by 30, with a draught of 3 metres, and at each corner had a retractable leg 50 metres long. After being towed

The Waves of Time

to its destination, the legs were let down, then the body of the barge climbed up the legs until it was raised high above the water-level. As descendants of the desert tribes, the people of the Emirates (especially their seafarers) were known for the virtue of patience. Where the oil industry is concerned, patience is not merely a virtue but an essential, for its lead times are long; four years elapsed from the Cousteau expedition to the point when *Adma Enterprise* commenced operations in January 1958. But thereafter success was swift. In March 1958, nearly 1700 metres below the seabed and 33 kilometres east of tiny Das Island, Abu Dhabi's first commercially viable deposits of oil were found.

Adma Enterprise being towed from Das Island after fitting out to the site of Umm Shaif No. 1 Well, 1958.

The site of the well, named Umm Shaif, was near the Great Pearl Bank, source of so much of the Emirates' former marine earnings. Whether it was a natural coincidence or a gift of God, if a line is drawn on a chart from Dhahran in Saudi Arabia through Qatar to Abu Dhabi city, the result is strikingly clear. Oil was found onshore at both Dhahran and Qatar. As the line continues towards Abu Dhabi, it runs straight through the middle of the Emirates' first major offshore oilfields. Their geology was not significantly different to that of the fields onshore – except that pearl-beds formed their roof and they might be anything up to 130 kilometres from the mainland. Though the translucent blue-green waters of the Gulf were not unmanageably deep, in the late 1950s and early 1960s such distance from land would have made commercial development of the oilfields highly uncertain, had it not been for the remote deserted island of Das. Offering a nearby landfall for submarine pipelines, the island – a geological freak, an arid salt plug a kilometre wide and less than 2 kilometres long, visited only by thousands of pairs of breeding migratory seabirds, marine turtles and the occasional fisherman – was a perfect partner to the oilfields. Without it, the Emirates' offshore oil industry, the new vital phase of its marine heritage, would have been long delayed.

A hard-hat diver preparing to descend to the seabed to inspect the site of a well, in 1957.

Nowadays it is hard to remember just how modest were the resources of the Emirates and, with the jet age in its infancy, the length of time required to journey from place to place. It took Susan Hillyard (the wife of Tim Hillyard, BP's first permanent representative in Abu Dhabi) three days to travel from the UK to the Gulf, landing on Dubai creek in a 'flying boat' in September 1954. Continuing by sea, the family (they had their baby daughter with them) arrived in Abu Dhabi during the night, and were startled to be shot at by a vigilant guard. At dawn they waded ashore. In Susan's words, 'Abu Dhabi boasted neither jetty nor road'. Nearly all the local

The Waves of Time

people lived in simple 'arish huts of bamboo and palm-leaf; and although a western-style house – the first in the Emirate – had been built for the Hillyards, all their fresh water came (weather permitting) 'by fishing boat from Dubai, in barrels which were rolled up the beach'. By the time the Hillyards left four years later, stores in Abu Dhabi stocked a variety of western foodstuffs, but to begin with, only a very limited range was available, and that from Dubai – Abu Dhabi had nothing of the kind to offer. Nevertheless, they thrived, because the diet was good. They lived, like everybody else, on a diet consisting mainly of rice, tomato paste, dates, chapattis, tea 'and excellent fish.' The fishermen, they discovered, could provide more than fish: as well as lobster and shellfish, the Hillyards were sometimes, as 'a rare and delicious treat', able to buy the meat of a dugong which had been accidentally entangled in the nets.

Airstrip, Das Island, Gulf Aviation Dakota in foreground, 1962.

New Wealth from the Sea

Steel towers for fitting around the well-head.

Tim Hillyard's function was to keep the Ruler of Abu Dhabi, Sheikh Shakhbut, constantly informed about progress in operations. Both men found it a matter of consuming interest, for offshore drilling was as new to BP as it was to the Emirate. One of the first concerns was to improve communications with the outside world, and in December 1954 Gulf Aviation, the forerunner of Gulf Air, carried out a proving flight onto Abu Dhabi's newly marked-out airstrip: a hard-packed section of sand edged, for the pilot's guidance, with petrol tins.

As the offshore industry began to take shape, fishermen, sailors and labourers all benefited from the new and expanding demand for their skills. It was said that at the time, the entire resident European population of the Emirates could have been seated around a single dinner table. If so, there was soon an empty place, for in 1956 Pat Townsend from BP (an important shareholder in ADMA) became the first permanent inhabitant of Das Island, setting up home in a small prefabricated hut left by the seismic surveyors. The island was to become an oil terminal, and the advantages to ordinary people of the Emirates were immediately apparent. Apart from birds and their eggs, there was nothing on Das to sustain human life. Everything had to be imported, and on the mainland, laid up only for lack of work, there were *dhows* by the dozen, together with experienced captains and crews. After years of enforced idleness, these elegant vessels became once again a common sight at sea, carrying all manner of materials to Das – and men, for nothing could be built without builders.

Following Townsend onto Das came expatriate workers from India and Pakistan, the first of whom promptly introduced cricket to the island – little risk there that rain would stop play; and of course numerous workers came from Abu Dhabi too. Some, as fishermen, had visited the island in its virgin state; some were from deep in the country's interior; some were former pearl divers. Much respected for their swimming abilities, these men would lay and relay underwater cables, and were among the many who now stayed as employees for ten years and more, periodically travelling to and from their homes on the mainland and enjoying for the first time in their lives the benefits of regular, stable work.

Golf provided some welcome relief from work, Das Island, 1962.

Barge carrying a section of a well-head tower approaching Adma Enterprise at the site of Umm Shaif No. 3 well, 1960.

Das developed very quickly. Fresh water was imported from Bahrain in ex-naval landing craft, which also brought heavy building equipment, notably bulldozers and explosives for quarrying the low hills at the north of the island. 'Arish huts and other accommodation, a hospital, workshops, and a mosque with a resident sheikh were soon installed, along with a sea-water desalination plant and all the spreading paraphernalia – pipes, pumps, storage tanks – of an oil terminal. At the south end of the island a harbour and an airstrip were built, while off the island, where the water was deeper, jetties appeared for tankers and other large vessels. Out to sea, Adma Enterprise erected permanent drilling rigs at one location after another; and in 1962, in the poetic phrase of a British annual report, 'the sheikhdom of Abu Dhabi crossed the portal of affluence'. On 11 June, with the lighting of Das's first flare of waste gas, the exploration phase ended. Three weeks later, on 4 July, the first cargo of crude oil from Abu Dhabi and from

The Waves of Time

the UAE as a whole was exported from Das. The sea was providing once again. Through the late 1950s and early 1960s the extent of Umm Shaif was steadily uncovered. Within a decade of the drilling of well No. 1, more than 30 other productive wells had been drilled at strategic intervals over the enormous field. In the same period, the even larger Zakum field had been found (1964) halfway between Umm Shaif and Abu Dhabi city and, west of Das, the small Bunduq field (1965). Both were linked, like Umm Shaif, to Das. The island was rapidly becoming one of the most industrialised patches of land in the Gulf – possibly in the world – yet it remained host to migrant nesting seabirds. Because of the diminished available space, their numbers were reduced from the tens of thousands that used to congregate and breed there, but in the early months of each year, great flocks of terns still soared and swooped above the glittering silvery reflections of hydrogen sulphide plants, storage tanks and separators.

From 1996 onwards, hundreds of pairs of white-cheeked terns began once again to nest on Das, raising their young beneath the gas flares. Why the birds chose to return after an absence of over 30 years is unknown, although their new and unexpected breeding success is a fascinating example of the way in which nature and man can co-exist in even an unpromising environment.

The growth of the terminal at Das was mirrored by the dramatic growth of its human population. Within ten years, there could be, on any given day, up to 1600 men living and working on the island, with others being flown to and from the island on a daily basis. They were taught a wide range of practical skills – written and spoken English, welding, driving, motor servicing, typewriting, morse, radio communications, meteorology, machine-shop engineering, the control of powerhouses and geological analysis – and increasing numbers were able to take up advanced education. One of the first to do so, typifying the national transition, was Khalfan Khalifah, whose father grew dates in the summer and caught fish in the winter. In 1961, at the age of 14, he had come to Das to sweep laboratory floors, and was so inspired by the scientific work he saw that in due course he graduated in Britain as a chemical engineer.

Covering 80 per cent of the UAE, it is not surprising that Abu Dhabi was the first to discover oil, and its production and reserves too are in proportion to its size. Dubai, the second largest of the Emirates, was also the next to find oil (1966) in the Fateh field. As with Abu Dhabi, this was offshore and Sharjah followed in 1972, with the discovery of the Mubarak field – once again offshore. Inevitably, though, Abu Dhabi attracts the most attention, and there, two enormously important steps were taken with the commissioning, in 1976 and 1978 respectively, of the Umm Shaif and Zakum supercomplexes. Described as 'ships that never move, pinned to the coral' (or more prosaically as 'factories on stilts in the middle of the ocean'), the supercomplexes involve numerous platforms linked by bridges. From the platforms, treated water is injected into the wells to increase the subterranean pressure and enhance production; and rising to the platforms comes not only crude oil but gas. Reduced to liquid form by refrigeration and pressurisation, gas was first exported from Das in 1977. Doing so brought a double environmental benefit: firstly, the flaring-off of waste gas could be progressively reduced; secondly, liquefied natural gas (LNG, primarily methane) is exceptionally clean and efficient as a fuel. And we cannot overlook another consequence of the Emirates' LNG exports because, looming over the *shu'ais* and *belems*, it introduced one of the most sophisticated class of ships – the dedicated LNG tanker, designed to keep its cargo chilled to less than minus 165 degrees Celsius – to the world's marine heritage as well as to its own.

The United Arab Emirates has changed enormously since the Cousteau expedition, the ADMA *Enterprise* and everything that followed (although it is only fair to point out that Abu Dhabi's first of many major onshore oil discoveries, at Bab, took place no more than a year after the successful first well at Umm Shaif) yet, as noted at the beginning of this chapter, in many ways the continuity with the past is even more remarkable than the changes. This continuity relates in part to the former scarcity of natural resources which implanted the knowledge that to exploit nature without care or conscience is to ignore the needs of the future. Such awareness means that while the relationship of the people of the UAE to the sea and its new-found riches has undergone a dramatic transformation, its marine heritage is richer today than it ever has been, because the UAE maintains a vigilant stewardship in order to conserve its existing gifts for as long as possible. Occasionally there have been effortlessly fortuitous and unexpected benefits. For example, the submarine sections of all those offshore wellheads and supercomplexes were not particularly intended to be successful breeding-grounds for mussels and other small shellfish, but they have become so. Similarly, their related underwater structures – pipelines and breakwaters – have become the foundations of new coral reefs, as nature colonises that which man has put in place.

Key marine habitats in the UAE, such as Khor Kalba, which is home to the endemic white collared kingfisher, receive Government protection.

The dedicated policy of conservation which operates in the UAE is mainly due to one man. Back in 1953, an employee of BP described His Highness Sheikh Zayed bin Sultan Al Nahyan, youngest brother and representative in Al-Ain of the Abu Dhabi Ruler of the day, Sheikh Shakhbut bin Sultan as

a charming man with a great sense of humour, and clearly a very powerful character. He is largely responsible, by his personal example and his prestige among the Bedouins, for the fact that Abu Dhabi in its present form has survived so long as it has. It appears to be generally considered that Zayed would make an admirable successor to Shakhbut. Were he to succeed it might well be that, by his force of character and by a wise use of the revenues available to him, the present independence of Abu Dhabi might be consolidated.

The description was not only perceptive but prophetic, for Sheikh Zayed succeeded his brother as Ruler on 6 August 1966, and, following the creation of the United Arab Emirates in 1971, he became president of the union. Since then, building upon their separate pasts, Abu Dhabi and its six sister Emirates have jointly maintained not only their independence from other states but also their shared maritime traditions. Pearling has disappeared with little prospect of revival, except as a way of preserving memories of the past heritage, but other marine industries which had been failing – particularly fishing, shipbuilding and shipping – have experienced a renaissance. Completely new marine-related services have been put in place, and the UAE's coastal waters are now a focus of attempts to promote marine environmental conservation, an important consideration in one of the busiest waterways in the world.

Without the oil industry, none of these would have been possible. Offshore oil has itself become an integral part of the marine heritage, but, no less importantly, it has enabled the people of the Emirates to uphold and develop the older aspects of that heritage – aspects which otherwise would have faded into history. Fishing was one of the first marine industries to benefit as the population grew after oil was found. The UAE fish catch is now one of the largest per head in the Arabian peninsula. although due consideration is now also being given to the dangers of possible over-fishing. Along with the rising revenues from oil came a revival for the traditional shipbuilding industry, and there are active yards in Abu Dhabi and Ajman.

Benefiting more directly from the offshore oil industry is a modern shipbuilding and ship-repair industry. The Dubai Drydocks, for example, can cater for the world's greatest oil tankers, while numerous shipyards, including the joint venture Abu Dhabi Shipbuilding Company, owned partly by US firm Newport News, build, equip and repair a variety of vessels for the offshore supply industry. Fabrication of offshore drilling rigs, accommodation platforms and pipelines is now an important part of the UAE's heavy industry, with products being used not only in the country's own offshore waters but being exported extensively to other countries in the region.

Thus today, the effects of the UAE's offshore oil industry can be felt far more widely than in the oilfields themselves and in the national exchequer. From fishermen to engineers and architects designing the massive offshore structures, from traders meeting the demand for supplies for the staff of the rigs and terminals to port stevedores offloading the incoming goods, all owe a part of their livelihood to this new and vibrant sector of the country's marine heritage.

Indeed, without oil, that heritage might well have entered a terminal decline. Though oil and the revenues from it have provided the wherewithal for development, however, the will and the wisdom to use it properly came from elsewhere. In 1966, shortly after becoming Ruler,

Sheikh Zayed stated as one of his basic principles that 'Oil is useless if it is not exploited for the welfare of the citizen.' It was a view which he would reiterate frequently and with remarkable consistency, saying more than 20 years later, 'If God Almighty has bestowed wealth upon us, our first obligation in expressing our gratitude should be to direct this wealth to the country's reform and to provide welfare to its people.' And again, speaking in 1996 on the twenty-fifth anniversary of the foundation of the UAE: 'Wealth in itself is of no value unless it is dedicated to the prosperity and welfare of the people.'

In August 1954, between Cousteau's visit and the first well on the Umm Shaif field, a British journalist pondered the future of the Trucial Coast (as the Emirates were still called) and the possible effect of a major oil strike. Oil, in his view, was 'the most modern of money-makers and troublemakers. It could place their perpetual truce under severe strain. Water would be a greater boon than oil.' Ironically, it is precisely because of oil that the UAE is now well supplied with water. God's gifts do not always come in the most obvious form.

St Paul's Cathedral in London houses a famous inscription in memory of its architect: 'If you want to see his memorial, look around you.' Something similar could be said of the offshore oil and gas industry in the UAE, for although much of its activity takes place far out of sight of land, either hidden in the heat-haze or beyond the horizon, it is inextricably woven into every aspect of life in the federation.

Dug from the desert, Jebel Ali is the largest man-made harbour in the world.

Select bibliography

Chapter One

Brindley, H.H. 'Early Pictures of Lateen Sails', *The Mariner's Mirror* 12 (1926) pp 9-22.

Graeve, M.-C. de. *The Ships of the Ancient Near East (c. 2000–500 B.C.)*. Leuven, Orientalia Lovaniensia Analecta 7 (1981).

Grupe, G. and Schutkowski, H. 'Dietary shift during the 2nd millennium BC in prehistoric Shimal, Oman peninsula', *Paléorient* 15/2 (1989) pp 77-84.

Johnstone, P. *The Sea-Craft of Prehistory*, London and Henley, Routledge & Kegan Paul (1980).

Littleton, J. and Frøhlich, B. 'Fish-eaters and farmers: Dental pathology in the Arabian Gulf', *American Journal of Physical Anthropology* 92: 1993) pp 427-447.

Ministry of Information and Culture. *Oman, a seafaring nation*, Muscat (1979).

Possehl, G.L. 'Meluhha', in J. Reade (ed), *The Indian Ocean in Antiquity*, London: Kegan Paul International, 1996) pp 133-208.

Potts, D.T. *The Arabian Gulf in Antiquity*, i. Oxford: Clarendon Press (1990).

Potts, D.T. 'Watercraft of the Lower Sea', in U. Finkbeiner, R. Dittmann and H. Hauptmann (eds), *Beiträge zur Kulturgeschichte Vorderasiens: Festschrift für Rainer Michael Boehmer*, Mainz: von Zabern, (1995) pp 559-571.

Potts, D.T. *Mesopotamian Civilization: The Material Foundations*, London: Athlone and Ithaca: Cornell (1997) (esp. Chapter V. 'Watercraft').

Ray, H.P. 'Maritime Archaeology: The Ethnographic Evidence', *Man and Environment* 21 (1996) pp 74-85.

Salles, J.-F. 'Achaemenid and Hellenistic trade in the Indian Ocean', in J. Reade (ed), *The Indian Ocean in Antiquity*, London, Kegan Paul International, (1996) pp 251-267.

Stephan, E. 'Preliminary report of the Faunal Remains of the first two seasons of Tell Abraq/Umm Al Quwain/United Arab Emirates', in H. Buitenhuis and H.-P. Uerpmann (eds), *Archaeozoology of the Near East II*, Leiden: Universal Book Service (1995) pp 52-63.

Vogt, B. in J. Reade (ed), 'Bronze Age maritime trade in the Indian Ocean: Harappan traits on the Oman peninsula', *The Indian Ocean in Antiquity*, London, Kegan Paul International, pp 107-132.

von den Driesch, A. 'Viehhaltung, Jagd und Fischfang in der bronzezeitlichen Siedlung von Shimal bei Ras al-Khaimah/U.A.E.', in P. Calmeyer et al. (eds), *Beiträge zur altorientalischen Archäologie und Altertumskunde: Festschrift für Barthel Hrouda zum 65. Geburtstag*, Wiesbaden, Harrassowitz (1994) pp 73-85.

Chapter Two

Gawlikowski, M. 'Palmyre et l'Euphrate', *Syria*, 60 (1983) pp 53-68.

Gropp, G. 'Christian maritime trade of Sasanian age in the Persian Gulf', in K. Schippmann et al. (eds), *Golf-Archäologie*, Buch am Erlbach, Internationale Archäologie 6 (1991) pp 83-88.

Hirth, F. *China and the Roman Orient: Researches into their ancient and mediaeval relations as represented in old Chinese records*, New York, Paragon (1966) (repr. of 1885 ed).

Hourani, G.F. 'Direct sailing between the Persian Gulf and China in Pre-Islamic times', *Journal of the Royal Asiatic Society*, (1947) pp 157-160.

Krenkow, F. 'The Annual Fairs of the Pagan Arabs', *Islamic Culture* 21/2 (1947) pp 111-113.

Potts, D.T. 'Arabia and the kingdom of Characene', in D.T. Potts (ed), *Araby the Blest: Studies in Arabian Archaeology*, Copenhagen, Carsten Niebuhr Institute Publications 7 (1988) pp 137-167.

Potts, D.T. *The Arabian Gulf in Antiquity*, ii. Oxford, Clarendon Press (1990).

Potts, D.T. 'The Parthian presence in the Arabian Gulf', in J. Reade (ed), *The Indian Ocean in Antiquity*, London: Kegan Paul International, (1996) pp 269-285.

Potts, D.T. 'The Roman relationship with the *Persicus sinus* from the rise of Spasinou Charax (127 BC) to the reign of Shapur II (AD 309–379)', in S. Alcock (ed), *The Early Roman Empire in the East*, Oxford, Oxbow Monographs 95 (1997a) pp 89–107.

Potts, D.T. 'Late Sasanian armament from Southern Arabia', *Electrum* 1 (1997b) pp 127-137.

Potts, D.T. and J. Cribb. 'Sasanian and Arab-Sasanian coins from Eastern Arabia', *Iranica Antiqua* 30 (1995) pp 123–137.

Shoufani, E. *Al-Riddah and the Muslim Conquest of Arabia*. Toronto, Univ. of Toronto Press (1972).

Sudzuki, O. 'Silk Road and Alexander's Eastern Campaign', *Orient* 11 (1975) pp 67-92.

Teixidor, J. 'Un port romain du désert: Palmyre', *Semitica* 34 (1984) pp 4-127.

Van Neer, W. and Gautier, A. 'Preliminary report on the faunal remains from the coastal site of ed-Dur, 1st–4th century A.D., Umm al-Quwain, United Arab Emirates', in H. Buitenhuis and A.T. Clason (eds), *Archaeozoology of the Near East I*, Leiden, Universal Book Services (1993) pp 110–118.

Zhang, J.Y. 'Relations between China and the Arabs in Early Times', *Journal of Oman Studies* 6/1 (1983) pp 91-109.

Chapter Three

Ahmad, N. 'Moslem Contribution to Astronomical and Mathematical Geography', *Islamic Culture*, 18 (1944).

Arnolds, T.W. Sir, 'Arab Travellers and Merchants, 1000-1500 A.D', in A.P. Newton (ed) *Travels and Travellers of the Middle Ages*, London, (1926).

Baramki, D. Sumer 31 (1975).

Barbosa, D. 'The Book of Duarte Barbosa: an account of the countries bordering the Indian Ocean and their inhabitants', *Hakluyt Society*, 2nd series, Vol.39 (1918-21).

Beaujouan, G. and Poulle, E. 'Les origines de la navigation astronomique aux XIVe et XVe siecles' in Mollat, M. (ed), *Le Navire*, Travaux du 1er Colloque d'Histoire Maritime Paris, SEVPEN (1957).

Beech, M. 'Ancient Marine Resource Exploitation in the Arabian Gulf', forthcoming Ph.D. thesis

Bensaud, J.A. *L'astronomie nautique au Portugal a l'epoque des grandes decouvertes*. Berne, (1912).

Bowen, R.L. *Arab Dhows of Eastern Arabia*, Massachusetts (1949).

Bowen, R.L. 'Primitive watercraft of Arabia', *American Neptune*, 12 (1952).

Bowen, R.L. 'Eastern Sail Affinities', *American Neptune*, 13 (1953).

Boxer, C.R. *Four centuries of Portugese expansion, 1415-1825*, Berkeley (1969).

Boxer, C.R. *From Lisbon to Goa 1500-1700: Studies in Portuguese maritime enterprises*. London (1984).

Brice, W.C. 'Early Muslim Sea Charts', *Journal of the Royal Asiatic Society*, (1977).

R.J.C. Broadhurst (ed), *The Travels of Ibn Jubayr* (1145-1217), London (1952).

Chaudhuri, K.M. *Trade and Civilization in the Indian Ocean*, Oxford (1985).

Cipolla, Carlo M. *Guns, sails and empires: Technological innovation and European expansion 1400-1700*, (1965).

Collinder, P.A. and May, W.E. *A History of Marine Navigation*, Henley on Thames (1973).

Cortesao, A. *Cartographia et Cartografos Portuguesos dos seculos XV-XVI*. Lisboa (1935).

Cotter, C.H. *History of Nautical Astronomy*, London (1968).

Da Mota, T.A. 'Methodes de navigation et cartographie nautique dans l'Ocean Indien avant le XVIe siecle', in *Ocean Indien et Mediteranee*, Sixieme Colloque Int. de Histoire Maritime, Paris, SEVPEN (1964).

Danvers, F.C. *The Portugese in India*, New York (1966).

Da Albuquerque, A.1774 edition, 'The Commentaries of the Great Alfonso de Albuquerque' trans. Birch, W.d.B. *Hakluyt Society* (1875).

De Cardi, B. Doe, D.B. 'Archaeological survey in the Northern Trucial States', *East and West* 21 (1971).

Dulles, F.R. *Old China Trade*, London (1970).

Edwards, C.R. 'The impact of European overseas expansion on ship design and construction during the sixteenth century', *Geojournal*, 26: 4 (1992).

Elders, J.A. 'The excavations of the Nestorian monastic settlement at Sir Bani Yas island, Abu Dhabi Emirate 1993-96', unpublished archive report (1997).

Fatimi, S.Q. 'In search of a Methodology for the History of Muslim Navigation in the Indian Ocean', *Islamic Quarterly*, 43 (1978).

Ferrand, G. *Relations des Voyages et textes geographique arabes, persans et turcs relatifs al l'extreme Orient, du VIII au XVIII siecle*, Paris (1913).

Ferrand, G. *Instruments nautiques et routiers arabes et portugais*, Paris. (1921).

Ferrand, G. *Introduction a l'astronomie nautique arabe*, Paris (1928).

Gibb, H.A.R. (trans), *The Travels of Ibn Battuta* (abridged), London (1929).

Gibb, H.A.R. (trans), *The Travels of Ibn Battuta*, Cambridge (1958, 1962, 1971).

Hardy-Guilbert, C. *Julfar, cite portuaire de Golfe arabo-persique a la periode islamique*. Paris (1991).

Hart, H.H. *The Sea Road to the Indies*. New York (1950).

Harvey, P.D.A. *Medieval maps*, London (1991).

Hawkins, C.W. *The Dhow, an illustrated History of the Dhow and its world*, Lymington. (1977).

Hellyer, P. *Arabian Wildlife*, (1997).

Hornell, J. 'A Tentative Classification of Arab Seacraft', *Mariner's Mirror*, 28 (1942).

Hourani, G.F. (reprint), *Arab seafaring in the Indian Ocean in Ancient and early Medieval Times*, Princeton (1995).

Howard, D. *Dhows*, London. (1977).

al-Idrisi, Mohammed ibn Mohammed. 'Kitab nuzhat al-mushtaq fi iqtiraq al-afaq', in A. Bombaci, U. Rizzitano, R. Rubinacci, L.V. Vaglieri, (eds), *Opus Geographicum*, Naples and Rome.

Janssen, M., 199/. ////////

Jewell, J.H.J. *Dhows at Mombasa*. Nairobi (1969).

Johnson, T.M. and Muir, J. 'Portuguese influences on shipbuilding in the Persian Gulf', *Mariner's Mirror*, 48 (1962).

Kennet, D. 'Jazirat al-Hulaylah - early Julfar', *Journal of the Royal Asiatic society* 4, 2 (1994).

Kennet, D. 'The Towers of Ras al-Khaimah' BAR 61 (1995).

Kennet, D. 'The excavations at Kush', *Arabian Archaeology and Epigraphy* 27 (1997).

King, G.R.D. 'Excavations by the British team at Julfar. Report on the third season (1991)', *Proceedings of the Seminar of Arabian Studies*, 22 (1992).

King, G.R.D. Dunlop, D., Elders, J.A. 'The Abu Dhabi Islands Survey', *Proceedings of the Seminar for Arabian Studies* 24 (1994).

King, G.R.D. (1996).

King, G.R.D. (1997).

Lewis, A.R. 'Maritime Skills in the Indian Ocean 1368-1500', *Journal of the Economic and Social History of the Orient*, 16 (1973).

Lishman, N. 'Arabian Lateeners', *Mariner's Mirror*, 47 (1961).

Lorimer, J.G. *Gazeteer of the Persian Gulf, Oman and Central Arabia*, Vol II, Geographical and Statistical, Calcutta (1908).

Moore, A. 'Craft of the Red Sea and Gulf of Aden', *Mariner's Mirror*, 6 (1920).

Moura, C.F. 'Portuguese Caraveloes', in R. Reinders, and K. Paul, (eds), *Carvel Construction Technique* Oxford (1991) pp 190-194

Miller, K. *Mappae Arabicae*, Stuttgart (1926).

Nafis, A. 'Moslem Contribution to Geography During the Middle Ages', *Islamic Culture*,17 (1943).

Nakhili, D. *As-Sufun al Islamiyah*, Alexandria (1969).

Navdi, S.S. 'The early relations between Arabia and India', *Islamic Culture*, 11 (1937).

Potts, D.T. *The Arabian Gulf in Antiquity*, Vol I, II. Oxford (1992).

Prestage, E. *The Portuguese Pioneers*, London (1933).

Richards, D.S. (ed) *Islam and the Trade of Asia*, A Colloquium, Oxford (1970).

Salih Shihab Hasan, *Fan al-Milahah Inda-Arab*, Beirut (1982).

Sasaki, T. 'Vietnamese, Thai, Chinese, Iraqi and Iranian Ceramics from the 1988 sounding at Julfar', *Al-Rafidan* 12 (1991).

Somogyi, J.D. *A Short History of Oriental Trade*, Mildesheim (1968).

Stanley, H.E. *The Three Voyages of Vasco de Gama*, London (1869).

al-Tabari, Mohammed ibn Jarir, *Annales*, Leiden (1879-91).

Tibbets, G.R. *Arab Navigation in the Indian Ocean before the Portuguese. Royal Asiatic Society, Oriental Translation fund*, New series, vol.XLII. (1971).

Tolmacheva, M. 'On the Arab system of Nautical orientation', *Arabica*, 27 (1980).

Villiers, A. *Sons of Sinbad - An Account*, London (1940).

Villiers, A. *Monsoon Seas - The Story of the Indian Ocean*, New York (1952).

Wilmshurst, D. 'The Syrian 'Brilliant Teaching'', *Journal of the Hong Kong Branch, Royal Asiatic Society*, Vol.30 (1990).

Yajima, H. 'The Arab Dhow trade in the Indian Ocean: A preliminary report', *Studiae Culturae Islamicae*: 3. Tokyo (1976).

Yakut, ibn Abd Allah al-Hamawi, *Kitab mu'jam al-buldan*. H.F. W. Stenfeld (ed), 6 Vols, Leipzig (1924).

Zaniel, A.S. 'The Dhows of Kuwait. Conservation of a Tradition. Part 1: Construction of the Ship', *Journal of the Institute of Wood Science*, 9.3 (1982) pp139-144

Zhang Jun-Yan, 'Relations between China and the Arabs', *Journal of Oman Studies*, Muscat.

Chapter Four

Tibbetts, G.R., *Arab Navigation in the Indian Ocean before the Coming of the Portuguese*. The Royal Asiatic Society of Great Britain and Ireland, London (1981).

Chapter Five

Heard-Bey, F. *From Trucial States to United Arab Emirates*. Longman, London and New York, (1996).

Chapter Six

Dawson, L.S. *Memoirs of Hydrography*. First published in 1885; Facsimile edition London (1969)

Brucks, George Barnes, 'Memoir Descriptive of the Navigation of the Gulf of Persia', *Selection from the Records of the Bombay Government*, No XXIV. Bombay (1856) pp 532-634.

Cook, Andrew (ed.), *Survey of the Shores and Islands of the Persian Gulf 1820-1829*. 5 Vols. Archive Editions. Slough, (1990).

Horsburgh, James, *The India Directory, or Directions for Sailing to and from the East Indies*, (6th ed), London (1852).

Markham, C.R. *A Memoir of the Indian Surveys* (2nd ed 1878).

Payne, Anthony. 'A Newly Discovered Chart by John Friend' *The Map Collector*, Issue No. 53, Winter (1990) pp 38-9.

The Persian Gulf Pilot, Taunton (1982).

'Remarks on the Navigation of the Persian Gulf, by Captain John Wainwright of His Majesty's Ship *La Chiffone* in the years 1809 & 1810', The United Kingdom Hydrographic Office, Miscellaneous papers, Vol. 64, which also contains similar remarks by George Crichton former 1st Lieutenant of the *Chiffone*.

Chapter Seven

Aspinall, S.J. *Status and Conservation of the Breeding Birds of the United Arab Emirates,*, Dubai, Hobby (1996).

Heard-Bey, F. *From Trucial State to United Arab Emirates*. Longman (1982).

Heard-Bey, F. 'The Tribal Society of the UAE and its Traditional Economy' in E.Ghareeb, & I. Al Abed (eds), *Perspectives on the United Arab Emirates*, London, Trident Press (1997).

Hellyer, P. (in press) *Filling in the Blanks: Six Years of the Abu Dhabi Islands Archaeological Survey*.

Hellyer, P. (in press) *Hidden Riches: An Introduction to the Archaeology of the United Arab Emirates*.

King, G.R. 'The History of UAE: The Eve of Islam and the Islamic Period' in E.Ghareeb, & I. Al Abed (eds.). *Perspectives on the United Arab Emirates*, London, Trident Press (1997).

Potts, D.T. Before the Emirates: An Archaeological and Historical Account of Developments in the Region c5000 BC to 676 AD. In: E.Ghareeb, & I.Al Abed, (eds), *Perspectives on the United Arab Emirates*, London, Trident Press (1997).

Scott, D.A. (ed). *A Directory of Wetlands in the Middle East*, IWRB/IUCN, (1995).

Index

Photographic Credits

Bridgeman Art Library, London, 6-7, 88-89, 98, 102, 131

D.T. Potts, 9, 11, 19, 20, 21, 22, 27, 28, 36, 37, 49, 50, 55, 56, 57, 58, 62

Trident Press/Hanne and Jens Eriksen, 14, 16, 25, 29, 33, 44-45, 69, 101, 103, 151, 158, 167, 179, 180, 181, 182, 152-153, 165, 179, 180, 181, 182

G.R.D. King, 65, 66, 81

Simon Aspinall, 12 -13, 16, 18

Trident Press/Adam Woolfitt, 41, 128, 132, 133

John Nowell, 71, 95, 113, 125

British Library, London, 73, 76

Royal Geographical Society, London, 75, 93, 137

Ronald Codrai, 79, 82, 84, 85, 86-87, 97, 106, 117, 118, 119, 124, 126, 127, 160

Oriental and India Office Collections, London, 90-91

Trident Press/Charles Crowell, 105, 183

Trident Press/Alex Smailes, 115, 121

Archives of the Abu Dhabi Company for Onshore Oil Operations (ADCO), 120 (3 photos), 122, 159, 161, 168

Archives of the British Petroleum Company p.l.c. (BP), 123, 170, 171, 172, 173, 174, 175, 176

Peter J. Vine, 129, 162

Details and views on the following pages are reproduced by permission of the Controller of Her Majesty's Stationery Office and the UK Hydrographic Office, 138, 139, 140, 141, 142, 143, 144, 145, 146, 147, 148 (2 Photos) 149

Jurgen Freund, BBC Natural History Unit, 154

Linda Pitkin, 155

Jeff Rotman, BBC Natural History Unit, 157

Jeff Collett, 161

Hanne and Jens Eriksen, 163, 177